WALKING ON
THE WILD SIDE

WALKING ON THE WILD SIDE

Long-Distance Hiking on the Appalachian Trail

KRISTI M. FONDREN

RUTGERS UNIVERSITY PRESS
New Brunswick, New Jersey, and London

Library of Congress Cataloging-in-Publication Data
Fondren, Kristi McLeod, 1975–
Walking on the wild side : long-distance hiking on the
Appalachian Trail / Kristi M. Fondren.
pages cm
Includes bibliographical references and index.
ISBN 978–0–8135–7189–8 (hardcover : alkaline paper) — ISBN 978–0–8135–7188–1
(paperback : alkaline paper) — ISBN 978–0–8135–7190–4 (e-book : Web PDF) —
ISBN 978–0–8135–7570–4 (e-book : ePub)
1. Hiking—Social aspects—Appalachian Trail. 2. Hikers—Appalachian Trail—
Biography. 3. Hikers—Appalachian Trail—Social conditions. 4. Subculture—
United States—Case studies. 5. Self-actualization (Psychology)—Case studies. 6.
Appalachian Trail—Description and travel. 7. Appalachian Trail—Biography. 8.
Appalachian Trail—Social conditions. I. Title.
GV199.42.A68F65 2016
796.510974—dc23   2015004956

A British Cataloging-in-Publication record for this book is available from
the British Library.

Visit our website: http://rutgerspress.rutgers.edu

Manufactured in the United States of America

What are these, so wither'd and so wild in their attire,
That look not like th' inhabitants o' th' earth, And yet are on't?

—William Shakespeare, *Macbeth*

CONTENTS

ACKNOWLEDGMENTS

Many people have contributed to the creation of this book. First and foremost, I thank the forty-six men and women who shared with me their experiences hiking the Appalachian Trail. I also express my gratitude to the many trail angels I encountered while hiking portions of the trail. Their unexpected acts of kindness, from rides to kind words, to offers of a shower or a hot meal, always came when they were needed most.

The many individuals and institutions that provided assistance during the research and writing of this book also deserve my thanks. Of particular significance is the assistance of John Bartkowski and Duane Gill. Dr. Bartkowski has been a wonderful mentor and friend throughout this process, from my days as a graduate student to the realization of this book, and for that I will always be grateful. Had it not been for Dr. Gill's course in environmental sociology, I may never have become a sociologist. I will always remember his passion for this line of research. Appreciation is also due to Lynne Cossman and Nicole Rader. I am also grateful to the following at Mississippi State University for their financial support: the College of Arts and Sciences, the Department of Sociology, the Gender Studies Program, and the National Strategic Planning and Analysis Research Center (particularly Steven Grice and Domenico Parisi).

To my colleagues in the Department of Sociology and Anthropology and the Center for Teaching and Learning at Marshall University, I thank you for your support and encouragement throughout the writing of this book. I also thank my department chair, Marty Laubach, for his continued support, and Sherri Smith for her helpful advice. I am grateful for funding from the following at Marshall University: the Department of Sociology and Anthropology and the College of Liberal Arts (particularly Dean Robert Bookwalter).

I also thank my editor at Rutgers University Press, Peter Mickulas, for his support and encouragement of this project. He helped make this book a reality and was always available when I had a question. Special thanks as well to the anonymous reviewers of my manuscript for Rutgers University Press; they offered invaluable feedback on the manuscript. And a special thank you to Alan Graefe and John Bartkowski for their most helpful reviews. Their detailed communication and close reading of chapters contributed to the completion of this project. For diverse smaller, but nonetheless crucial contributions, I thank the Rev. Dr. John Minihan for his thoughtful discussions and comments regarding religious pilgrimage, ritual transformation, and renaming found in biblical teachings. For other technical issues, I also appreciate Amber M. Wright for her detailed reading of chapters, as well as Elizabeth Martin for her assistance setting images.

Throughout this process, many friends and family sustained me and, at times, reminded me of life beyond academia. I thank my husband, Marty, for his patience and support during the writing of this book. I also thank my parents, Wayne and Merle McLeod, who have always encouraged me in pursuing my education and realizing my full potential. I cannot thank you both enough. I am particularly thankful to Deborah Harris and Chris Bounds as well for their continued friendship and support of this project since its inception while we were graduate students at Mississippi State. New friends have also provided encouragement and support throughout this process. Thank you to Rachel Sparkman, Amanda Bartoe, Sara Johnston, Katelin Denkins, Kara Callison, and Rich Brinkman for continuing to encourage and challenge me, for hiking with me, or for tending to things at home when I was away hiking. Finally, for thirteen years of domestic love and distraction, I am thankful for my furry friends, Memnoch the Devil and Akasha Queen of the Damned. My deepest appreciation and thanks to all.

WALKING ON
THE WILD SIDE

1 ❧ FROM GEORGIA TO MAINE

The GA–ME Is Afoot

On a cloudy day in the middle of May, in downtown Damascus, Virginia, the atmosphere was ripe for battle. The lightning and thunder had passed. Just a few raindrops remained, softly falling on us—and them. It was us against them, always us against them. Men and women, young and old lined the sidewalks surrounding Main Street, winding all through downtown, around the corner, and over the bridge and beyond. They were armed. We were armed. It was time. They knew it, and we knew it. In the beginning it seemed almost peaceful. Some of the local citizens of Damascus appeared on their porches as we, a mighty mob of hikers, made our way down Main Street. It wasn't long before the first shot was fired. A water balloon. Then came the full-on attack. Water balloons, water guns, super soakers, and even the occasional water hose (see fig. 1). It was total chaos. Hikers left the parade temporarily and playfully fought with locals in their yards, all the while pelting and being pelted with weapons filled with water. Lady Mustard Seed, a twenty-six-year-old hiker from Florida, described this event as "a retreat to childhood" and "the rowdiest thing" she had ever experienced in her life up to this point. Children were screaming as they aimed water guns and sailed water balloons toward the mob of hikers. Laughter filled the air.

The town of Damascus, Virginia, with a population of 814, touts itself as the friendliest trail town on the Appalachian Trail. Each year in May approximately 10,000 people (locals, current and former long-distance

1. Water fight between community members and a group of hikers during the annual hiker parade at Trail Days, 2011. Photograph by author.

hikers, hiking enthusiasts, religious organizations, gear representatives, and more) descend upon the small town for the annual Trail Days festival. Trail Days is an event that reunites Appalachian Trail hikers and celebrates their journey with food, music, gear replacement or repair, documentary film screenings, showers, medical assistance, a hiker parade and talent show, and nightly drum circles around campfires at Tent City, a large camping area approximately one mile south of town. In many ways, Trail Days is similar to a high school class reunion. For the hiker parade, held on the Saturday of the festival, long-distance hikers come together and make banners for their hiking class—say, Class of 2001—which they carry in front of them as they hike through the town of Damascus during the parade (see fig. 2).

Hobo Joe, a twenty-two-year-old hiker from Massachusetts, considered Trail Days to be "one of [his] most memorable experiences." He remarked: "Once you're out here you really belong to this group of people. It's very exclusive in that way." Many hikers echo Hobo Joe's sentiments about Trail Days as a "highlight" of the Appalachian Trail experience, which is why

2. Members of the hiking class of 2001 carry their recently made banner as they head down Main Street during the annual hiker parade at Trail Days, 2011. Photograph by author.

many hikers, past and present, come back year after year to relive those experiences and renew friendships.

The stories of community and belonging as told by Hobo Joe represent a familiar pattern for many long-distance hikers on the Appalachian Trail. Trail Days is but one of many events or places along the Appalachian Trail that allow hikers to come together, creating a unique bond among members of this leisure subculture. For hikers like Drifter, a forty-four-year-old repeat thru-hiker from New Hampshire, the lifelong friendships he has made over the eleven years of hiking the Appalachian Trail and the shared experiences that he believes he can only have on the Appalachian Trail are what continue to bring him back to the AT, time and again.

In his 1958 book *The Dharma Bums*, beatnik Jack Kerouac wrote, "Think what a great world revolution will take place when . . . [there are] millions of guys all over the world with rucksacks on their backs tramping around the back country." The numbers have not quite reached "millions," but thousands of men and women, old and young, have developed an interest in long-distance hiking. Compared to the relatively short-term activity of day hiking or overnight hiking, long-distance hiking (or backpacking) requires multiple days and nights on a trail while carrying camping gear, food, and shelter (although sometimes shelters are provided in the form of three-wall lean-tos or four-wall huts).

Long-distance hiking did not begin to grow in popularity until 1970, driven in part by the release of Ed Garvey's book *Appalachian Hiker: Adventure of a Lifetime*. Between 1936 and 1969, the Appalachian Trail Conservancy recorded only fifty-nine completed hikes of the AT. In 1970, ten people, including Garvey, were recognized as "2,000-milers"—a term used to identify a growing group of hikers who set out to hike the entire length of the Appalachian Trail. In the decades that followed, the number of 2,000-milers increased dramatically, particularly during times of economic recession. In 2006 and 2007, two years before the most recent recession, there were 525 people recognized each year as 2,000-milers. Since the Great Recession, there has been a steady increase of approximately 40 to 90 additional 2,000-milers per year. Perhaps some individuals are looking to hike the Appalachian Trail as an escape from urban living and the fatigue and stress associated with it as they search for emotional or spiritual rescue related to job loss or limited job opportunities.

On August 14, 2012, America's 2,181-mile-long Appalachian Trail celebrated the seventy-fifth anniversary of its completion as the longest hiking-only footpath in the world. Often referred to as the longest and skinniest national park, the Appalachian Trail crosses fourteen states and more than sixty federal, state, and local parks and forests (see fig. 3). Marking the official route of this congressionally recognized National Scenic Trail are white paint blazes, two-inch-by-six-inch vertical rectangles, found in both directions and painted on everything from rocks and trees to signs, bridges, posts, or other objects approximately one-tenth of a mile apart.

The United States is home to eleven congressionally recognized scenic trails, nineteen historic trails, and over a thousand recreation trails. Other long-distance trails in the English-speaking world include fifteen national trails in England and Wales, and another four in Scotland. In the end, I chose the Appalachian Trail as my research site because it is arguably the most social and most frequented long-distance hiking trail. Overall, since 1936, the Appalachian Trail Conservancy has recorded slightly more than 12,000

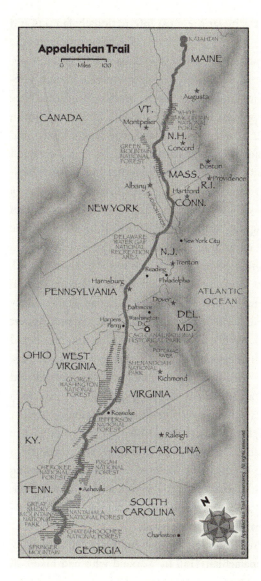

3. Map of the Appalachian Trail. Photograph courtesy of the Appalachian Trail Conservancy.

completed hikes made by thru-hikers (those completing the entire trail in one continuous journey) and section hikers (those completing the trail in large sections over a period of time). Of this number, a little more than two hundred hikers have thru-hiked the Appalachian Trail more than once.

Of those trails that make up the Triple Crown of hiking trails (that is, the Appalachian Trail, the Pacific Crest Trail, and the Continental Divide

Trail), the Appalachian Trail is by far the most internationally famous and most popular. According to the Appalachian Trail Conservancy, people from all over the world—Australia, Austria, the Bahamas, Belgium, Canada, Chile, the Czech Republic, Denmark, England, Finland, France, Germany, Holland, India, Ireland, Israel, Italy, Japan, Mexico, Morocco, New Zealand, Norway, the Philippines, Romania, Scotland, Singapore, South Africa, South Korea, Spain, Sweden, Switzerland, the Netherlands, and Wales—have reported hiking the Appalachian Trail. This phenomenon maybe due in part to the 1998 publication of travel writer Bill Bryson's best-selling book, *A Walk in the Woods: Rediscovering America on the Appalachian Trail*, wherein he humorously describes his attempt to reconnect with his homeland by thru-hiking the Appalachian Trail with his out-of-shape friend, Katz. This particular cultural representation of the trail by Bryson is reported by hikers and nonhikers alike, in the United States and abroad, as their first introduction to the Appalachian Trail. The influence Bryson has had on people's decisions to thru-hike the Appalachian Trail is likely to increase with the release of a movie based on his book, starring Robert Redford as Bryson and Nick Nolte as his buddy Katz. The film premiered during the 2015 Sundance Film Festival and was released in September 2015.

Unlike Drifter, the repeat thru-hiker from New Hampshire introduced earlier, the typical long-distance hiker is stepping onto the Appalachian Trail for the first time and has either recently graduated from high school or college or just retired. Most, however, are like Drifter in that long-distance hikers are predominantly single, white, male, educated, and come from working- and middle-class American families. Many admit to choosing to hike the Appalachian Trail because it is the most social and most well-known long-distance hiking trail in the United States compared to its cousins, the Pacific Crest and Continental Divide Trails.

Like most hikers, including Hobo Joe, Drifter, and Lady Mustard Seed, I was introduced to the Appalachian Trail by a friend who had hiked all of it, except Maine anyway. During summer 1999, I hiked approximately 350 miles in just over a month, from the Delaware Water Gap on the Pennsylvania–New Jersey border to Manchester Center, Vermont. Before this time I had been unaware of the Appalachian Trail, or its iconic status, and had never been long-distance hiking. This is not uncommon for a majority of long-distance hikers. When I returned to hike another portion of the trail in 2005, I had no idea that it would be the beginnings of a larger research project. I knew from my experiences in 1999 that the Appalachian Trail was a special place, a storied place. There was a unique community that formed among hikers as they made their way from Springer Mountain in Georgia to Mount Katahdin in Maine. So this time, and again in summer 2007, I figured that while I was out there hiking I might as well get to know the hiking community better.

Because I could talk the talk and walk the walk, it was not difficult for me to gain entry and become part of the long-distance hiking community on the Appalachian Trail. Everyone I approached was more than willing to speak with me about their trail experiences and relationships with fellow hikers. In fact, no one I approached declined to be interviewed. The majority of long-distance hikers I spoke with identified themselves as thru-hikers, meaning their intentions were to thru-hike the trail over the course of the next few months. I do not know how many of them actually made it to Katahdin. Most began hiking the trail in mid- to late March or early April. Although April Fool's Day is traditionally the first day for starting a northbound thru-hike, a few long-distance hikers started as early as February, which I am finding to be increasingly common.

Given that nearly four million people will set foot on the trail each year, the long-distance hikers I had the opportunity to speak with are not representative of all who hike or come to experience the Appalachian Trail. When I searched Amazon and Google, I found more than thirty-five memoirs in which hikers recounted their experiences of long-distance hiking, and that's only on the Appalachian Trail. Most recently, Cheryl Strayed chronicled her 1995 solo hike on the Pacific Crest Trail in *Wild: From Lost to Found on the Pacific Crest Trail* (2012). Her memoir received rave reviews and became the basis for a film of the same title starring Oscar-winning actress Reese Witherspoon. The film was released in December 2014 in select locations. The attention Strayed's book, and now movie, has brought to the growing activity of long-distance hiking has been referred to by media outlets as the "*Wild* effect," as hundreds of women hit the PCT, inspired to follow in Strayed's footsteps.

Although there have been quite a number of hiking memoirs published, this ethnographic project, in which I explore the long-distance hiking community on the Appalachian Trail, is the first in-depth research project of its kind. Recognizing that subcultures are best conceptualized and understood as products of social interaction, I focus on social relationships and social practices among members of the long-distance hiking community. My approach reveals that beyond exploring the social self, it is vitally important to examine the place-situated self. Environmental sociologist Kai Erikson (1994) stated in his studies of trauma and the human experience of modern disasters that personal investment in a place (home, for example) is not simply an expression of one's preferences or tastes but rather an expression of one's personality, a part of the self. Within the discipline of sociology, when speaking of the development of the self, sociologists generally focus on a socially situated self that is constructed in relation to significant others. Largely missing from this body of work is the notion that we are also place-situated beings, forming identities in relation to significant places, not solely from attachment to others.

The Appalachian Trail has been imbued with multiple meanings since the idea of the trail itself was first introduced in 1921 by Benton MacKaye. MacKaye's vision of the Appalachian Trail project was not the long-distance hiking trail known today but rather a practical vision for wilderness conservation in the Appalachian region. MacKaye believed that a series of recreational camps and community life, compared to modern society, would replace the dull, routine existence of the working class and become a sanctuary and refuge from the commercialism of everyday life (MacKaye 1921; Minteer 2001). In other words, MacKaye envisioned a trail that would become an alternative to urbanization and development rather than an adjustment to it (Foresta 1987). According to Ronald Foresta (1987), MacKaye's biggest problem was that his idea and his initial vision of the project came too late—the social structure and class outlook in the United States had changed. After 1918, there was no longer concern about improving life for the working class through social reform but rather how to accommodate the reality of industrial capitalism (Foresta 1987; Minteer 2001). There was no longer a direct attack on modern industrial society because industry created wealth for many sectors of society and increased the range of consumption opportunities for citizens, including the consumption of leisure activities (Foresta 1987).

Another reason the Appalachian Trail project failed to be an instrument of social reform for the urban working class was that MacKaye and early reformers did not provide the leadership necessary for such a project (Foresta 1987; Minteer 2001). Initially a cooperative venture guided by social reformers, the Appalachian Trail project fell into the hands of professionals guided by public land managers, all of whom were encouraged by industry and benefitted from the opportunities an emerging industrial society had to offer (Foresta 1987). Headed by Myron Avery, this new leadership established the first Appalachian Trail Conference (renamed the Appalachian Trail Conservancy in 2005). The primary focus of the ATC was on trail construction and design, and coordinating the volunteer activities of local hiking clubs (Foresta 1987). Avery and his associates were typical of those who became active in the Appalachian Trail project after MacKaye. They were young, educated professionals—public land managers, foresters, lawyers, professors, physicians, editors, and scientists—whose activities and interests in the Appalachian Trail were separate from their vocations, a pattern common among middle- and upper-class Americans of that era. Since most of the trail builders were professionals and had secure jobs, they were not as concerned with the social ills of the day but instead viewed nature as a temporary escape from society. They believed the Appalachian Trail would allow individuals an opportunity to enjoy the material benefits of the city as well as the spiritual and physical conditioning of the great outdoors (Foresta 1987).

Today, the Appalachian Trail is a primitive environment in which long-distance hikers can become temporarily separated from modern society. Moreover, certain features associated with long-distance hiking help promote a unique place-situated identity for members of the hiking community. Some of those conditions are the geographical, physical, and social isolation from mainstream society; continuous contact with other long-distance hikers, directly or indirectly; the exceptional difficulty, danger, and variability of the trail; and the necessity of being and living on the trail on a daily basis for an extended period of time. Additionally, places and events along the Appalachian Trail, such as Trail Days mentioned at the beginning of the chapter, provide opportunities that encourage feelings of community and camaraderie among hikers. When I asked Swinging Jane, a sixty-three-year-old thru-hiker from Ohio, what her highest point had been so far, she mentioned trail towns or other places on the trail itself. For her, "the Damascus area was a high point, and Silar Bald was a high point. . . . The Mount Rogers experience was something that I'll eventually go back and do again. Grayson Highlands and seeing the ponies. I think all of those were high points." As Spirit, a fifty-seven-year-old section hiker from Tennessee, put it, "You may not be religious but you are going to go through something on this trail."

For most long-distance hikers, like Swinging Jane, Spirit, and others introduced earlier, the Appalachian Trail represents a meaningful place whose power is unfolded in the stories long-distance hikers share about their trail experiences. This study is the first of its kind to adopt a holistic approach to investigating the construction of a place-based identity. Although my sample is not necessarily representative of the entire long-distance hiking community, my focus on long-distance hikers on the Appalachian Trail reveals the presence of a multilayered leisure subculture. As part of this study, I compiled basic statistics about age, race, class, gender, and education; I was, however, less interested in quantifiable conclusions than in the narrative of the lived experiences of long-distance hikers.

Doing ethnographic fieldwork and conducting in-depth interviews with long-distance hikers provided me an opportunity to give voice to a group of hikers who have largely been ignored in leisure and recreation studies. While I am familiar with this body of research, I will spare the reader an extended discussion and simply say that most research on hiking in the area of recreation management has focused on it as a short-term, daily activity rather than as an extended, long-term one (see Kyle et al. 2003; Kyle, Bricker et al. 2004; Kyle, Graefe et al. 2004; Manning et al. 2000). In fact, no systematic study of which I am aware has been conducted on the extended activity of long-distance hiking or backpacking other than those studies relating backpacking to a form of tourism (see Cohen 2003; Cohen 2011; Shaffer 2004). Moreover, prior research has demonstrated that long-distance hikers (both thru-hikers and section hikers) on the Appalachian Trail develop a stronger socio-emotional connection to the AT compared to other types of hikers (such as overnight/weekend and day hikers).

Of the four million visitors who will set foot on the Appalachian Trail in a given year, only about 2 to 3 percent identify themselves as thru-hikers. Due to this small number compared to other types of hikers, earlier studies have often excluded thru-hikers from the research pool. This is unfortunate in that thru-hikers spend more time engaging with the Appalachian Trail than anyone because of the extended amount of time they spend on the trail. Their engagement with the trail suggests they are more likely to develop an attachment or emotional bond to it. Because thru-hikers spend roughly four to seven consecutive months hiking the trail, it would be expected that the social relationships thru-hikers develop with others would be stronger and positively affect their desire to hike. So, I ask, does hiking versus long-distance hiking or backpacking offer the same recreational experience? This research highlights how the physicality and experiences of hiking and long-distance hiking differ for recreationists engaged in these activities, as well as when they are engaged with a particular leisure setting over an extended period of time.

In this volume, I argue that the Appalachian Trail is valued for its ability to provide recreationists with opportunities for social interaction and deep connections to place. An emerging body of work asserts that in contemporary society, as our identities have become increasingly fluid and fragmented (Elias 2000; Holyfield and Jonas 2003), individuals have begun to construct identities from multiple sources, including sport and leisure lifestyles (Dant and Wheaton 2007; Hunt 1995; Wheaton 2000; Wheaton and Beal 2003; Wheaton and Tomlinson 1998; Williams and Donnelly 1985). More specifically, sports considered new or "extreme"—such as windsurfing, skateboarding, canoeing, deep-sea diving, skydiving, and rock climbing—have been viewed as a product of postmodern society and culture, offering a basis for the construction of new and multiple identities (Bradley 2010; Wheaton 2000; Wheaton and Beal 2003). Although this research on leisure subcultures and subcultural identities is rich and varied, scholars have yet to consider the extended leisure activity of long-distance hiking as a source of identity.

One goal of this project is to write about the lives of long-distance hikers, both on and off the Appalachian Trail, from their perspective. Long-distance hikers live in isolation, for the most part, and have their own ways of acting, talking, and thinking; their own vocabulary; their own activities and interests; their own concept of what is significant in life; and to a certain extent their own scheme of life. Typically, such immersed practices lead to a more intense form of social intimacy and bonding as a result of shared experiences. This volume evaluates and offers an understanding of relationships that form among long-distance hikers as they collectively construct a long-distance hiker identity through their social practices and shared experiences on the Appalachian Trail.

I argue that the experiences and relationships that emerge among long-distance hikers while on the Appalachian Trail provide hikers with a unique subcultural identity, one that often remains with them after their time on the trail is over. After their trail experience, long-distance hikers must reenter the society they left behind. This transition is often marked by an initial period of culture shock, stress, and depression due to the physiological changes that occur when a person is no longer hiking day after day, as well as the emotional aspects that follow when that person is separated from the community and freedoms enjoyed on the Appalachian Trail (Bruce 2006). Eventually hikers who have escaped the confines of society and multiple identities must return to struggle with them, including the newly developed trail identity, and may experience difficulty negotiating between their new trail identity and their former identities. This research project suggests that long-distance hikers on the Appalachian Trail not only develop a long-distance hiker identity but also a trail identity, an identity that is formed in relation to this particular recreational setting.

In studies of leisure and recreation, place identity is defined as a component of self-identity, or a constellation of patterns of ideas, beliefs, preferences, feelings, values, goals, and behavioral tendencies and skills relevant to a specific recreational setting (Proshansky 1978). Although previous research on leisure subcultures has identified subcultures that form around a particular activity, no previous study has examined the impact of a particular leisure setting in the construction of a subcultural identity. In other words, although, say, a windsurfing subculture has emerged and windsurfers may consider places like the Columbia Gorge important, no specific body of water has been identified as holding significant meaning for members of a "windsurfing subculture." Whereas many of the studies investigating the extent to which recreationists become attached to certain leisure settings have only done so with regard to the relationship between the person and the recreational activity, a central feature of this research is the marriage of place and activity in the development of a long-distance hiker identity.

So, how does the long-distance hiking subculture on the Appalachian Trail sustain itself? Typically, subcultures are transmitted and sustained through face-to-face interaction among members, but hikers on the Appalachian Trail are in a constant state of flux. As a result of variations in hiking pace, miles hiked per day, occurrence and extent of injuries, length of stays in towns, direction of one's hike, as well as point of entry, long-distance hikers often do not interact with the same people on a daily basis, making the constant reinforcement of social norms virtually impossible. Additionally, no formal institutions exist on the Appalachian Trail for socializing individuals into a long-distance hiking subculture. Because of this absence, flows of information are not automatic but must be channeled and mediated by other means. This volume investigates the processes though which inexperienced hikers are introduced and socialized into the long-distance hiking subculture in the absence of sustained face-to-face interaction.

In short, this ethnographic study focuses on a series of significant questions facing scholars, as well as those in charge of management over natural resource–based recreational settings:

- How do the leisure activities of hiking and long-distance hiking or backpacking differ?
- How do we understand the long-distance hiking community in terms of the sociality and social practices of its members?
- What impact do recreational settings have in the formation of leisure subcultures and subcultural identities?
- How does the long-distance hiking subculture sustain itself in the absence of continued face-to-face interaction?

Drawing on key insights from subcultural studies and identity theories (see Stets and Burke 2000; Stryker 1991; Stryker and Serpe 1982; Tajfel 1970; Tajfel and Turner 1986; Turner et al. 1994), this work focuses on understanding how a situated hiker identity is collectively informed and negotiated among members of the long-distance hiking community as boundaries are established through social practices, or the "doing" of activities. Following a boundary work perspective (see Lamont 1992, 2000), I explore the various strategies used by long-distance hikers as they create boundaries to distinguish themselves from other types of hikers, such as overnight and day hikers. This approach allows me to examine patterns of inclusion and exclusion or ways that long-distance hikers construct similarities and differences among themselves and others.

Although countercultures are known by their rejection of mainstream society, many subcultures selectively borrow from mainstream society, twisting certain aspects to suit their own purposes. From a cultural studies perspective, Ken Gelder (2007) provides a useful framework for analyzing subcultures. He argues that subcultures, in their many forms, are first and foremost social and should be understood as such. In terms of the long-distance hiking community, the discussion that follows illustrates how this all works out for hikers on the Appalachian Trail.

In chapter 2 of this volume, I focus on the leisure subculture of long-distance hiking by examining the construction of a generic long-distance hiker identity and identifying common characteristics shared by all long-distance hikers regardless of hiking trail. More specifically, long-distance hikers can be identified through a range of distinctive behaviors such as excessive food consumption, self-discipline, an unwavering trust in complete strangers, a chosen life of poverty, and a rejection of modern-day structures. Long-distance hikers can be identified by their unkempt appearance, which often leads to a stereotype or perception of hikers as lazy and unwilling to work. Finally, long-distance hikers share a common language or system of communication, referring to one another by trail names, most of which come about from interaction with other hikers.

In chapter 3 I focus more specifically on a geographically situated subcultural identity, a long-distance hiker identity that emerges while hiking the Appalachian Trail. For example, there are many places and activities along the trail—including trail towns, hostels, hiking festivals, and shelters—that carry special meaning for long-distance hikers. These places help create social bonds among hikers who share these trail experiences. This investigation reveals that once on the Appalachian Trail, long-distance hikers develop a trail persona or trail identity in a locus where old identities become new identities. For many long-distance hikers, the Appalachian Trail represents a sacred place, a place to which they become attached socially and emotionally. Migration on and off the trail, as well as "reentry" back into society after their hike is over, serves to reinforce this geographically situated identity for a majority of long-distance hikers. Although they acknowledge that there are multiple long-distance hiking trails, many long-distance hikers on the Appalachian Trail suggest that the AT has a healing property to it and often return time and again to relive their experiences. Place, culture, and sacredness are thoroughly interconnected here for long-distance hikers. Thus, the extended activity of long-distance hiking on the Appalachian Trail can be characterized as an embodied experience for many.

The spiritual character of long-distance hiking is the focus of chapter 4. Qualitative research focuses on articulating worldviews, motivations, and narratives from the perspectives of study participants, so the tone of chapter 4 comes from the participants themselves as opposed to my own spiritual values. In this chapter, similarities between the extended activity of long-distance hiking and religious or Christian pilgrimage are discussed. For both hikers and pilgrims, the act of walking a great distance ends with a final, climatic goal—for most AT hikers, this means reaching the northern terminus, Maine's Mount Katahdin. When long-distance hikers first set foot on the Appalachian Trail, they find themselves in the liminal phase of pilgrimage—a space or moment in which one is suddenly marginal or decentered, where one experiences a change in state or social position (Turner 1974).

Relationships that develop among members of the hiking community can best be characterized as communitas relationships (personal and immediate); the nature of long-distance hiking, however, may determine that these relationships end as quickly as they are formed. In the early stages of the journey, the majority of hikers go through a renaming or conversion process whereby they adopt a trail name, one that for many is symbolic of their reasons for hiking the trail. Long-distance hikers may carry sacred texts or books of instruction to guide their journey. Such books may also offer directions for behavior and may help in navigating the trail. Along their journey, long-distance hikers stay in hostels and are celebrated by former hikers and trail angels who assist them along the way. This chapter also reveals that when fellow hikers come together at "sacred" sites, they dance, tell stories of adventure, of rituals and hiker traditions, of trail magic, or talk about the many heroes and legends of the Appalachian Trail.

Although it may seem as if long-distance hikers are a homogenous group, the Appalachian Trail does not represent a perfect utopian society, where everyone gets along free of inequality and hierarchical structures. In chapter 5, I illuminate the veiled inequalities and hierarchies that emerge among long-distance hikers as they hike the Appalachian Trail. To an extent, class, race, gender, and age are selective of those who participate in this extended recreational activity. The typical long-distance hiker is a white, educated, middle-class male in his twenties or late forties or older. Although long-distance hikers do not have a class-based identity and are without class consciousness, as understood in a traditional sociological sense, class—in addition to race, gender, and age—operates in the background by influencing participation. These social cleavages are present on the Appalachian Trail by their very absence.

This investigation also reveals the emergence of a hiker hierarchy on the Appalachian Trail, one distinguished by type of hiker: thru-hiker, section hiker, weekend or overnight hiker, or day hiker. Thru-hikers are at the top of the hiker hierarchy, followed by section hikers, weekend or overnight hikers, and day hikers. In addition to the hiker hierarchy, long-distance hikers are further stratified as a group on the basis of their approach to hiking—that is, a purist, white-blazer, blue-blazer, yellow-blazer, pink-blazer, flip-flopper, slackpacker, northbounder, southbounder (these terms are explained in chap. 5). Put succinctly, the social world of long-distance hikers can be characterized as structured, as well as individualized and competitive. For members of this leisure subculture, membership, identity, and status are not only shaped by one's approach to hiking, but by point of entry and the direction of one's hike.

The concluding chapter of this book distills key insights from the previous chapters. Here, I draw together key lessons learned about American society from the in-depth, ethnographic study of the sociality and social practices of long-distance hikers on America's most internationally well-known and most social long-distance hiking trail. This chapter identifies a long-distance hiking leisure subculture and explores how long-distance hikers come together over shared goals and experiences on the Appalachian Trail to create a uniquely situated subculture of place. Current surveys concerning recreation on the Appalachian Trail are primarily focused on hiking. Survey research on recreational use and leisure settings, specifically the Appalachian Trail, would benefit by distinguishing between the recreational activities of hiking and long-distance hiking. Thus, once managers understand why and how recreationists develop attachments to specific recreational settings like the Appalachian Trail, agencies can better design programs and maintain settings consistent with users' level and type of attachment (for instance, the regulation of long-distance hikers through Great Smoky Mountains National Park). I conclude this chapter by discussing the transmission and sustainability of a long-distance hiking subculture in a noninstitutionalized environment in the absence of continued face-to-face interaction.

You may have wondered, who is the "I" as I write? Throughout this book, the "I" appears in different guises—some I have chosen (researcher, ethnographer of hikers, long-distance hiker), and some were given to me by others (section hiker, Little One, Professor Little One). All of these represent the various identities that came to be as I immersed myself in the hiking community on the Appalachian Trail. Somewhere in between then and now I have sought to give voice to long-distance hikers as they recount their relationships and experiences hiking the Appalachian Trail. So, turn the page and join me and my fellow hikers as we begin the journey from Georgia to Maine. After all, the time is now. The GA–ME is afoot.

2 ❧ HIKER TRASH

Constructing a Long-Distance Hiker Identity

"Beware! You are about to enter The Rollercoaster." This was our greeting as my hiking partner and I entered this section of the trail in northern Virginia. The sign ensures there is no mistaking this section of the Appalachian Trail, situated between Bear's Den Rocks, a hiker hostel maintained by Queen Diva, and the small historic town of Harper's Ferry, West Virginia. It had been only five days since we started hiking, but they were five grueling days, half of which were spent on the infamous Rollercoaster. Over the next fourteen miles, we encountered at least a dozen PUDS (pointless ups and downs) as we climbed a total of 3,900 feet. We survived, but our knees were in pretty bad shape. All we wanted at this point was a shower, a hot meal, and a bed to sleep in for the night. As we began looking for signs indicating a hostel was near, a man caught us in his stare. With his tall, thin build, his white goatee, and a faded bandana tightly wrapped around his head, he was almost a dead ringer for Osama bin Laden. Were it not for his carpenter's belt, we might have been fooled. As he walked over, he greeted us with "You look like butt, you smell like butt, you're coming to my place." We laughed and laughed. My hiking partner and I spent that weekend in May with Bonzo, his dog Rio, and his girlfriend at their home in Harper's Ferry.

As it turns out, Bonzo, forty-eight-years-old at the time we made his acquaintance, had thru-hiked the trail in 1997 with his best friend and companion Rio, and was now working with the Appalachian Trail Conservancy in Harper's Ferry, clearinghouse of information about the trail. We got to know Bonzo pretty well over the weekend. When I asked him if there was a commonality among long-distance hikers, he hesitated a bit. He attempted to answer the question by saying, "It's the outdoors," but then asked, "Has anybody been able to explain it to you?" In this chapter, I attempt to do just that: find the common thread among long-distance hikers and, in the process, explain what it means to be that hiker. Long-distance hiking can be characterized as a physical, often strenuous activity, an embodied experience if you will. And bodies, I argue, are significantly involved in the construction of a long-distance hiker identity.

In this chapter I attend to two topics involving the construction of a long-distance hiker identity. The first is that long-distance hikers actively engage in identity construction in the sense that their identity is "made" by the hikers themselves through various behaviors they engage in as they come to see themselves as part of a group. The second is that a long-distance hiker identity is also constructed by outsiders. In other words, those outside the long-distance hiking community "construct" or create images or representations of long-distance hikers that may have little to do with hikers' self-perceived realities. These two issues are dealt with simultaneously.

WHO ARE LONG-DISTANCE HIKERS?

During an interview at Partnership Shelter, commonly referred to as the Taj Mahal of shelters on the Appalachian Trail, Slack, a twenty-nine-year-old "houseless" (as opposed to homeless) man, suggested that it is "not normal" to "climb mountains day after day after day after day for months going up and down and up and down through heat and bugs and snakes and bears." When I further inquired if there were any characteristics shared by all long-distance hikers, Slack replied, "You've got to be a special kind of wing nut to be out here." Though individuals have many different reasons for hiking the Appalachian Trail, long-distance hikers have much in common that distinguishes them from the average person in mainstream society. They can be identified and understood through a range of attributes that are distinctive compared to the restraints and moderations of "normal" populations. It is almost as if long-distance hikers go through an "uncivilizing process" when they first start their journey.

POVERTY AS A PREVAILING CULTURAL STYLE

As a result of this temporary life of poverty, long-distance hikers have a discernible appearance in which dirt, too often accompanied with an identifiable stench or "funky smell," is a primary indicator of difference. Recall the friendly greeting we received from Bonzo upon our arrival in Harper's Ferry. We were immediately recognizable to him. We had not bathed in over a week and had dirt under our fingernails and in the creases of our skin. Our hair was matted to our heads. In other words, the appearance and dress of long-distance hikers is often viewed as extreme in comparison to the dress and appearance of "normal" people, who generally are bathed and not drenched in sweat. Branch, a missionary from Georgia, described her experiences in local communities and how her appearance may have influenced interactions with nonhikers:

> Prior to hiking you're used to people perceiving you one way. You're clean, you're sort of dressed well, you didn't wear that shirt yesterday usually, so you're used to that kind of stuff and you almost want to melt into the crowd as a nonhiker. But with a hiker, it's almost like you have a completely different persona. You're a nasty, smelly hiker. And that attracts some people and that definitely detracts other people. So you get people who are super excited to see you just because you are a hiker and you've got other people who would cross to the other side of the street just to stay away from you.

Branch reported that her experiences in towns were "a little odd" because she "was ready to be treated like a normal person" rather than "the smelly person you don't really want to go around in the grocery store." Like Branch, many long-distance hikers feel out of place in local communities, especially towns or areas where locals, and in some cases tourists, are not aware of the trail's proximity.

It seems as if the more time hikers spend on a trail, the less their appearance matters to them because social norms associated with appearance and hygiene are less important and less stringent in the context of long-distance hiking than they are in "civilized" society. When Spirit and I began talking about her average day on the trail, she remarked that at home she was used to being "prim and proper" and "showering every day and sometimes twice a day." She continued to discuss her home beauty regimen and how that compared to life on the trail:

> I fix my hair. I don't wear it in public unless my hair is just perfect. I wear dresses most of the time. This is not how I would want it to be but you learn. You learn to deal with it. I know last time when I went home after I'd hiked a while my kids told me "Mom, you've lost all modesty." You do, you lose. It's not that you lose it but you learn that it wasn't that important. Life goes on and you can't fret about the little things. I don't like being dirty all the time and stinkin' but you have to, you have to live like that.

Spirit found herself really enjoying nature and the solitude it afforded her even though she was often uncomfortable in her own skin because she was used to being clean and wearing dresses at home.

Most long-distance hikers have only one or two sets of clothes (shirts, shorts, socks) and usually have the opportunity to do laundry and shower every five to seven days. Even when hiking clothes are washed, however, sweat stains are still noticeable. Once one set is laundered in town, hikers may quickly take off the last set and wash them too, even if it means using another hiker as a shield and changing in the middle of a laundromat. Some hikers, however, choose not to do laundry or shower as often, nor do they wear deodorant. This behavior or social practice associated with long-distance hikers is in stark contrast to the importance placed on personal hygiene in modern society, as illustrated by the sweet fragrances of shampoo and body wash emitted by two day hikers as they passed me just shy of Partnership Shelter, approximately a quarter of a mile from the parking area at the Mount Rogers Recreation Area Visitor Center in southern Virginia. While dress and appearance certainly distinguish a long-distance hiker from a nonhiker, or even from day or weekend hikers, this difference has led to a negative evaluation of hikers by those outside the hiking community.

HIKER TRASH

Long-distance hikers and bikers of the Harley Davidson type commonly refer to one another as "hiker trash" and "biker trash" when their paths cross, often at a road crossing or over a beer in town. Not everyone, however, uses the term "hiker trash" in such a friendly way. Graceful, a twenty-five-year-old thru-hiker from Tennessee, recounted fellow hikers' stories of making their way into Erwin, Tennessee, where children on a passing school bus yelled, "Hiker trash, get a job." When I asked her if there was anything she would like to change or do away with on the trail, if it were in her power to do so, Graceful said it would be "the stereotype of hikers, because when we [hikers] come to a town a lot of people are afraid of the way we look." I further inquired as to what the stereotype of a long-distance hiker was, and Graceful replied, "That we're lazy bums, that we don't have a job, that we've quit our job." She believes this negative perception of hikers initially relates to their unkempt appearance, but she insinuated that some resentment may be due to hikers' lack of employment. To further illustrate her point, Graceful recalled an experience she had at a restaurant, in a local community near the trail, in which she was treated poorly by the person waiting on her. I asked if she felt the treatment went back to the stereotype of hikers being lazy and not wanting to work, to which she replied, "Yeah, or in that case I think, too, it was a hardworking community. I could tell, the woman, she was working hard and had probably worked long hours at this diner, and she saw me as being lazy and you don't work."

Graceful is not the only one who expressed this concern. In fact, many long-distance hikers interviewed believe they are perceived and evaluated negatively by those outside the hiking community because of their lifestyle of leisure. When I asked Rez Dog, a fifty-seven-year-old thru-hiker from Arizona attempting a second thru-hike, to describe his experiences in local communities, he said, "You walk by this big plant in Pearisburg, you know, and those people are going to work every day and here we are on kind of a permanent vacation. Sometimes I think they might resent us." Although he suspected that local community members might resent him for not working, Rez Dog also said that he had not experienced hostility when passing through local communities; again, this was not the case for everyone.

Socks, a fifty-three-year-old thru-hiker from Connecticut, recalled negative interactions with outsiders in Tennessee: "Some [hikers] feel like people are staring at them or they've said things to them. There were some places in Tennessee where they told us to be careful, that people would holler things at you from cars, and some people did experience that." When I asked if she knew why this might happen, Socks replied, "Someone said that the Appalachian Trail Conference or the National Park Service has taken some land that belonged to families." Socks continued to suggest that the land was taken from families who have lived in that area for generations and have mountains named after them. While land acquisition could be part of the problem, particularly in this area of Tennessee, so too is a hiker's appearance and perceived lifestyle of leisure as he or she ventures into local communities to do laundry, shower, or resupply food.

A majority of long-distance hikers are aware of this negative evaluation and confront the stereotype by challenging it directly. In my experience, some people hike long-distance to raise money for a cause such as breast cancer, neonatal hospital units, or service men and women with post-traumatic stress disorder. Others, such as evangelical missionaries, students, documentary filmmakers, and academic researchers, challenge the stereotype by taking their work with them on the trail. Still others do so by equating the physical and mental aspects of long-distance hiking as work in and of itself. We come back to this topic shortly.

THE BIGGEST LOSERS

This discussion of hygiene and appearance leads to another behavior associated with long-distance hikers—excessive food consumption. Long-distance hikers do not have the luxury of taking a variety of foods with them when hiking. Hikers only carry what they need, not necessarily what they desire. A typical long-distance hiker's breakfast might be oatmeal, hot or cold, and coffee, optional. For lunch, there is the traditional trail mix or energy bar, maybe some peanut butter or other source of protein needed to keep going throughout the day. Once camped for the evening, hikers bring out their fuel and stoves for a hearty meal of dehydrated or ramen noodles complemented by an assortment of flavored drink mixes. Not all long-distance hikers carry this exact daily meal, but most carry something similar because these foods are lightweight. In fact, hikers have often joked that Lipton must have a monopoly on food options available to hikers. It does not matter if a hiker is going for long-term or short-term resupply, the Lipton brand is a staple found everywhere, from hostels and convenience stores to the local grocery.

Though it may seem that long-distance hikers follow a strict diet of sorts, this is not really the case. In towns, anything goes. Kutsa, a twenty-eight-year-old thru-hiker from Israel, told me that one of the things she missed most upon returning home, other than being free, was "being hungry." She admitted to struggling with diets and weight all her life, then said: "Most hikers hate [being hungry], but me, since I'm always over-weight, I'm never hungry in my life, and here it's like you can eat whatever you want. First of all you're accepted by the other hikers because everybody accepts that you would eat. You lose weight even though you eat whatever you want so I mean it's all good, right? (laughs)." In a society where people are continually bombarded with diet plans and advised to moderate their food intake to maintain a healthy weight, the fact that hikers sometimes binge, eating and drinking whatever they want, and still lose weight is an example of extreme behavior. Of course, if hikers are not careful, their habit of excessive eating can follow them home, leading to weight gain.

For long-distance hikers, excessive amounts of food are often provided in the form of trail magic. For me the most memorable experience involving trail magic in the form of food occurred in southern Virginia. After hiking five miles to a road crossing, we were met with a greeting of "Hey hik-ers, orange juice or apple juice?" Afterward, we heard, "Well, would you like some breakfast?" Needless to say, we responded with a unanimous "Yes!" The group that met us were members from a local United Method-ist Church in Bastian, Virginia, where they would take us for breakfast, and a pastor and his family from Star City, Arkansas. Once in the van, I asked the pastor from Arkansas why they were doing this for hikers, and he replied, "It's what we think Jesus would do or want us to do." They were all wearing T-shirts with the letters A.T.O.M., which stood for Appalachian Trail Outreach Ministry. Just below the letters was a diagram of an atom, with hikers representing electrons. Once we arrived at the little white coun-try church, we were greeted with smiles and hugs. First they took our pic-ture, asked us to sign a register, and then sat us down at a table for nearly fifteen people. They had local honey, which one hiker ate by the spoonful. Then they brought us apple butter, coffee, milk, orange and apple juice, green beans, potato casserole, and egg casserole with salsa if desired. Next, they gave us sausage and biscuits, rolls, another vegetable casserole, spiced apples, homemade cinnamon rolls, and strawberry-rhubarb pie for des-sert. We were absolutely stuffed. Because long-distance hikers must carry everything on their backs, they carry only the bare essentials, and extra food or comfort foods are considered a luxury.

Once we returned to the trail, we had only hiked a small piece before we met the young pastor and his family again (see fig. 4). They had more juice and were grilling hotdogs and hamburgers for anyone who had missed breakfast or who still wanted to indulge. And we did. No one felt the slightest bit guilty either. According to the Appalachian Trail Conservancy's website, a hiker can burn as many as 6,000 calories per day. With respect to caloric intake and weight gain, long-distance hikers truly are the biggest losers.

VARIETIES OF HIKER DISCIPLINE

While their appearance, behaviors, excessive food consumption, and perceived lack of work ethic or lifestyle of leisure may give the impression that long-distance hikers are uncivilized and lazy, perhaps wild and untamed,

4. A young pastor and his family from Star City, Arkansas, who are part of an Appalachian Trail Outreach Ministry (ATOM), greet and give trail magic to hikers on the trail near Bastian, Virginia, in 2005. Photograph courtesy of Christopher W. Bounds.

this would be an incorrect assumption. Long-distance hikers are, for the most part, extremely self-disciplined and motivated. They have to be as the physical act of long-distance hiking itself (that is, backpacking and camping outdoors on a daily basis), and the discomfort and injury that occur, is difficult, and hikers must continue in spite of pain, the weather, or the terrain. Also, they continue in spite of participating in an activity considered unnatural compared to "normal" activities.

Hustler, a twenty-five-year-old thru-hiker from Colorado attempting a second thru-hike of the AT, provided some insight into all that is involved when hiking long-distance. When I asked him about the characteristics shared by long-distance hikers, he said he concurred with remarks made by the person who runs Kincorra Hostel in Hampton, Tennessee:

> He always says the first thing is that a thru-hiker is very task-oriented. They have a task at hand and they need to get to the next town. So you're very task-oriented and your task is to make it to Maine. They're very highly confident because who knows how many people say "you're hiking to Maine, you're never going to make it, whatever, that's too big, you're hiking two thousand miles, you're crazy." So you have to be very, very confident. The third thing he says is you're very logistically minded because there are a lot of logistics that go into it as far as planning where your gear drops are, food drops, how many miles between towns, where towns are set up at, where the water sources are, just a lot of logistics. . . . But that's his theory and I can't really think of how better to explain it than the way he does. I think he's had ten thousand hikers through his hostel and that's the conclusion he's come up with and I agree one hundred percent.

Along with the physical challenge of hiking comes self-discipline, perhaps to a greater degree than what is found in "normal" populations. Hustler, out on a second thru-hike, said the "key to hiking" is "to be comfortable being uncomfortable." Backpacking on a daily basis in rugged terrain is not a comfortable, plush experience. Taz, a twenty-one-year-old thru-hiker from Maryland, admitted her most challenging experience was pushing herself to keep hiking despite her injuries. When I asked her to elaborate, Taz replied:

> I've had a lot of problems. Coming down Blood Mountain I blew out my right knee and that bothered me for a couple of weeks. Then I was diagnosed with

Giardia in Robinsonville at the clinic there. I also went to the hospital again in Newport, I think it was. I had that for about two and a half weeks strong and it's still lingering. But everybody knows that I'm always sick or injured at some point (laughs). I've got tendonitis in my Achilles so it's just keeping going even though my body seems to be falling apart. I just love being out here. I want to be out here and I'm probably going to be crawling on my hands and knees saying "I'm gonna do it, I'm gonna do it."

Taz, through her dedication and commitment to continue in spite of injury, is a good illustration of the self-disciplined hiker. Unlike Taz, most people, especially day or weekend hikers, would stop hiking, self-medicate, and heal in the comforts of home rather than remain on the trail; like Taz, however, the majority of long-distance hikers continue hiking on a daily basis even if they are experiencing serious physical discomfort or injury. The pain and discomfort are accepted by dedicated long-distance hikers as simply part of the hiking experience. Because of the arduousness of the trail experience, and the pain and discomfort that can become a regular part of daily life, long-distance hikers tend to develop a particular gait or walk, commonly referred to as the "hiker's hobble." Although the hiker's hobble looks about the same for all of us, the reasons can vary—from blisters, to muscle or joint pain in the legs, to missing toenails. I am happy to report I lost only two toenails on my last trip—both from my pinky toes.

Not only are hikers self-disciplined with respect to the pain experienced while long-distance hiking, but they also continue hiking when exposed to various types of weather. While HeartFire, a forty-nine-year-old section hiker from Texas, found it "wonderful to be out here in the elements day in and day out," others struggled with the exposure at times, including HeartFire herself. During the course of my interview with Firefly, a twenty-four-year-old section hiker from Indiana, she said her most challenging experiences on the trail have been weather related. During those times when the cold was unbearable, she struggled to convince herself to stay on the trail rather than go home. Because Firefly was accompanying her husband, Hazy Sonic, for part of his thru-hike, it would have been easy for her to make the decision to go home as she could have left at any point, but she willed herself to remain on the trail.

Graceful spoke about how the weather, always unpredictable, could affect a hiker's emotions, often making or breaking a day. At times, she said, a brief rain shower can be invigorating, whereas on other days the rain is "just added punishment on top of the pain you are already feeling." When I asked Hatchet Jack, a recent high school graduate from North Carolina, about his most challenging experience, he described the following weather-related incident:

> I had a week of twenties lined up and I did a twenty-three-mile day, and I woke up and it was pouring down rain. I was like, I've got to do it. I felt motivated to go do it, and so I started hiking. I hiked ten miles, and it was pouring down rain the whole entire time. I go in this shelter to eat and get a little bit dry but you've got to go right back out there in it. I'm hiking, and everyone I know stopped in Pearisburg. The trail goes right through Pearisburg, and I had to keep going because I had just stopped in town. It was really seeing everybody else stay in town, and it's pouring down rain and cars are driving by and just seeing civilization and knowing that you could be in a warm room and then it turns to sleet as I started going up in altitude. Then it turned to snow, and it just got harder and harder. I was sliding going up the mountain trying to climb and it was extremely rough. It was extra work because when it started snowing I took two steps and it counted as one. When I got to the end of the day it was just exhausting. It was one of the first times that I was hiking as fast as I could and I was still chilled. Usually you can hike and be warmed up immediately, but I was hiking as fast as I could and I was still chilled because everything I had was soaking.

Hatchet Jack's experience illustrates the self-discipline displayed by many long-distance hikers. He could have stopped with the rest of the group in Pearisburg, stayed dry, and let the weather pass. Alternatively, he could have stayed at the first shelter and only hiked ten miles that particular day. Either of these options is what any "normal" person would have done; Hatchet Jack, however, was determined to meet his goal of hiking a string of twenty-mile days. At least Hatchet Jack's water did not freeze, as it had for Yard Sale in the Smoky Mountains, an experience he referred to as a "life or death" situation. The only things that kept Hatchet Jack and Yard Sale moving were perseverance, commitment, and dedication, all characteristics associated with long-distance hikers.

Hatchet Jack's decision to continue on despite the weather is shared mostly by those hiking mainly for the physical challenge. T-Mac, a twenty-eight-year-old thru-hiker from Virginia, admitted he was out solely for the physical challenge. When I inquired how his reasons to hike the Appalachian Trail compared to those of other hikers, T-Mac said, "It's about fifty–fifty. Fifty percent are out here for the same reason, the challenge of making it from Maine to Georgia. The other half are out here just because they love hiking (laughs). They love hiking a lot (laughs)." T-Mac seems to capture the essence of the motivation for many long-distance hikers—they hike long distance as a way to challenge themselves or to reach a goal, or they simply love the outdoors.

Those hikers who are goal-oriented seem to be the hikers who push themselves in spite of the weather or physical pain and discomfort. Those who are out because they enjoy hiking or love the outdoors seem to focus on living more in the moment. As Montreal, a thirty-five-year-old repeat thru-hiker from Canada, commented, "A lot of rock bands like Pink Floyd criticized the fact that people are living a life for their pension or their retirement or it's always the goal and not the journey. And on the trail they always say the journey is the thing, not the goal." While some hikers, like Montreal, may be living in the present moment rather than thinking about the future or reliving the past, most long-distance hikers are task-oriented, or at least have to be a little, if they are going to make their ultimate goal.

THE GREAT ESCAPE

For individuals who are planners, long-distance hiking can feel like an enormous amount of work. As Skywalker, a forty-four-year-old thru-hiker from Georgia, remarked, "Everybody out here is working pretty hard. I mean this can be work. Challenging themselves. Extending themselves." And though this association with work may not faze some hikers, it can be extremely bothersome to others. For example, Kodak, an eighteen-year-old thru-hiker from New Mexico, had negative feelings toward work of any kind. When I asked her what her most challenging experience had been on the trail thus far, Kodak recalled a time when she was hiking "a string of days that were a little bit too long" for her. She said the worst moment came when she "sat down and [thought] this is just like a job. I get up every morning and I hike until I drop and I get up and I do it again. When I thought the words 'it's like a job,' that was the absolute worst." Kodak had recently finished high school and was intentionally delaying entry into the workforce.

Like Kodak, many long-distance hikers seek the wilderness because they hope to escape the structured world of work or because they are unhappy with their jobs. For example, Phoenix Rising, a thirty-two-year-old thru-hiker from Arizona, indicated she was miserable at her job. When asked if that had played a role in her decision to hike the Appalachian Trail, she replied, "Oh definitely. I realized that my job, I was basically supplying insurance for a bunch of rich people who owned airplanes, and it wasn't very rewarding and it wasn't very gratifying. I had been thinking about, questioning what I was doing and why I was there for a while." For work-related reasons, Phoenix Rising was at an airport when she came across Bill Bryson's *A Walk in the Woods*. She said reading Bryson's tale of adventures on the Appalachian Trail renewed a childhood dream of thru-hiking the trail. And since she was miserable at her job, Phoenix Rising made the decision to thru-hike the next summer.

Another common thread that emerged during my interviews with hikers was a rejection of the pressure to conform to structured routines and schedules in general. This theme became most apparent to me when hikers spoke about their experiences in Great Smoky Mountains National Park. Socks, a middle-aged thru-hiker from Connecticut, recalled that due to the difficulty of the trail in the Smokies, making it through that section was one of her highest points; it was, however, also an experience she had not liked because she had felt rushed. When I inquired as to why, Socks responded, "There were parts that would have been nice if you could have stayed another night there but you couldn't. They just regulate how many people. They need you to move on because of other people." Because many long-distance hikers are out for personal or spiritual reasons, they want to hike at their own pace without feeling rushed. For Socks, being regulated through the Smokies did not allow her to "hike her own hike." Slick, a twenty-three-year-old bartender from Florida, experienced similar frustrations in the Smokies. When I asked her if there was anything she would change about the Appalachian Trail, Slick quickly replied:

> The only thing so far that I've really begrudged was in the Smokies. The Smoky Mountains were beautiful but the way they've got that system set up . . . I don't know. It's just frustrating because you're going through there and they're so strict and there's like all these rules in the Smokies that they've

got set up so you can't stay, you can't set up your tent—most of us like to tent unless there's bad weather—like I can't sleep very well in the shelters anyway. The only time I sleep in the shelters is when it rains. And in the Smokies, it's like you have to stay in the shelter, and once the shelter is full, then you can tent right around the shelter. But, the problem is that they reserve for section hikers. Like you know 75 percent of the space is out or reserved for section hikers and then the rest is for thru-hikers. And if the section hikers don't show up, then the thru-hikers have to fill those spots.

Slick offered an example to further illustrate her point:

Like say there's eight reservations for a shelter and the three or four thru-hiker spaces that are reserved are already, someone's filled them, and you show up and you want to set up your tent because the ridge runner says there's eight reservations so the shelter by reservation should be full. If you set up your tent and they don't show up, you've got to break down your tent and get into the shelter. Or, on the flip side which is even worse, say you go, "Okay fine I'll get in the shelter"—because they won't let you set your tent up until the shelter is full—say you get into the shelter and the section hiker that has a reservation comes in at midnight for some reason, then you have to get out and set your tent up. I mean we had one night where we got snowed in, and you're not supposed to spend more than one night in [each shelter in] the Smokies, and the ridge runner was trying to tell us we had to go. We were all wearing trail runners. We didn't have boots and one guy had already tried to leave in trail runners and tried to break snow and he came back saying, "I'm going to get frostbite." And this guy was trying to tell us we had to leave. It just, I don't know. There were a lot of politics about the Smokies that I didn't like a lot, but other than that, it's all been great.

For the most part hikers do not have to conform to authority figures or rules when hiking long distance, which is one reason for Slick's frustration. Hikers are no longer punching a time clock and are not responsible for or dependent on anyone other than themselves. Aside from experiencing the vicissitudes of weather, hikers perceive themselves to be in complete control of their lives. Returning to a work-oriented or rule-governed environment like Socks and Slick encountered in the Smoky Mountains can be frustrating for long-distance hikers.

Although the daily tasks involved in hiking can become routine or monotonous, even controlled or structured by outsiders, many long-distance hikers find themselves on a trail because they simply need to escape. Bonzo thoughtfully added during an interview in his home in Harper's Ferry that this level of escape cannot be found anywhere except on the trail because "you don't have the influence of radio, television, newspapers, your nasty neighbor, your boss. I mean it's you and whatever you hear which is nature, the smell, the energy." Like Bonzo, many hikers believe that they can only find this level of escape or uninterrupted time to think about their lives in the wilderness. In fact, an overwhelming majority of long-distance hikers are at a transitional stage in life and searching for deeper meaning.

Happy Feet, a thirty-year-old thru-hiker, spent the last eight years of his life working as a network administrator for a paper company in Tyler, Texas, and did not like the "political battles" or the "corporate yucky" that his work environment had become. One of Happy Feet's co-workers told him about a book titled *A Walk across America* by Peter Jenkins. According to Happy Feet, Jenkins grew up in a snobby, rich environment in Connecticut and decided to hike across America to see if there were "different people" than those he grew up around back home. He hiked south from Connecticut, stopping in towns along the way to work and make money. During his walk, he became a Christian, met his wife, and then hiked from New Orleans to the Pacific Coast with her. Happy Feet was inspired by Jenkins's story and wanted to do something similar. He thought about traveling along railroads but decided to do a Google search to see what he might find. As he was searching for something meaningful to do with his life, he came across the Appalachian Trail.

Lady Mustard Seed also talked about how she needed to come into the wilderness to "figure out some things" in her life. I inquired about barriers at home that might keep her from finding the answers she was searching for, to which she replied:

> Your whole life in town is focused on sustaining your life in town. We work forty plus hours a week to sustain a certain lifestyle and that lifestyle is exhausting. It's hard to work forty hours. After I work my job I'm exhausted on the weekend. I don't have the energy to give back to my family, to myself, to God. And retreating into the woods, just leaving all of these obligations, leaving everything behind specifically just to seek and just to be with nature is

just a complete shift in focus. And it's a retreat into God and it's a retreat into nature whereas I feel like I'm spinning my wheels in town just trying to get the rent paid, just always rushing, you know, always tired.

As long-distance hikers remove themselves from the working world and the multiple roles or identities they occupy in society, spending time on the trail gives them a chance to sort through their lives. Not only does long-distance hiking provide a refuge from societal distractions for hikers searching for meaning, thus reinforcing a long-distance hiker identity, but it also provides an opportunity to settle unresolved personal issues without the daily distractions associated with home and work. Rez Dog, for example, was a hiker who had served in Vietnam, a war that he opposed. During my interview with him, he mentioned that any time he hiked he would think about his Vietnam experience since walking in the woods felt the same to him as walking in the jungle. Because his previous hiking trips had been shorter day hikes, he had never allowed himself to resolve his feelings about the war. When the thought came up he "could always put it aside because of job, family, or whatever." Rez Dog said he was eventually able to face this demon while hiking long distance because there were no other responsibilities to occupy his mind.

One of Rez Dog's most memorable moments on the trail came unexpectedly when he passed the Audie Murphy Memorial. Audie Murphy, the most decorated veteran of World War II, died when his plane crashed in the mountains near Roanoke, Virginia. The Veterans of Foreign Wars erected a monument in his honor near the crash site. Rez Dog recounted the following experience:

Probably one of the seminal moments of the hike was when we went by the Audie Murphy Memorial. And I sat and looked at that, and I'm real cynical about that sort of thing, and I read that and it was hard to be cynical about it. Looking at all those decorations, one of which was a combat infantry badge which I also have. And I finally realized that he and I are brothers. Even though the wars were different and how we participated were different, we are brothers in that. It was the first time that I ever had that sense of brotherhood and pride in my service. Seeing all of those decorations, I could stand back and salute and suddenly realized I am a veteran. I did serve and for the first time I felt a sense of pride even though I felt I did nothing for my country.

By the time I got to Virginia, central Virginia, that pretty much, I said, I did the best I could.

Rez Dog was able to resolve his feelings over the Vietnam War as he hiked the trail. When he was at home he could always put his thoughts about the war aside, but on the trail, when passing the Audie Murphy Memorial, he was unable to do so and, in the end, was able to resolve a personal issue that had been weighing on him a long time. So, it can be argued that this leisure activity provides motivation to leave societal "negatives" behind and fully focus on developing oneself without the distraction of outside influences.

Geronimo, a twenty-five-year-old thru-hiker who had recently left the military, decided to hike long distance to remove himself from the negative influence of "the media, the TV, the news," while Sweet Sixteen, a sixty-three-year-old section hiker from Michigan, wanted to do something "that was not negative." When I inquired as to why she had decided to hike the trail, she said, "America is so full of fear it just seemed . . . I wanted to do something unusual, something different . . . and not be afraid." As hikers remove themselves from the daily cares, concerns, and "negatives" of society, they have time to think and reflect without the influence of others or the distractions of everyday life. Golgi, a college student from North Carolina, shared his most memorable experience concerning the natural environment: he recalled a specific moment at the top of Max Patch when the beauty of nature reminded him how great life is and how, at times, that can be easy to forget because "of all of the consumerism and materialism we leave behind." Many long-distance hikers, like Golgi and others mentioned earlier, view consumerism, materialism, and media influence as negatives in society.

Long-distance hikers also mentioned feeling confined to a structured, routine world of work, which was a reason many found themselves hiking the Appalachian Trail. Yet the perception of long-distance hikers as lazy and unproductive does not reflect hikers' self-perceived realities. Still, the majority of long-distance hikers are at a transitional stage in life, one that for the most part seems to be work related. As Turbo, a twenty-four-year-old thru-hiker from North Carolina, stated, "A lot of people—some admit it and some don't—but I think a lot of people just want to put their life on hold. Maybe they're in the same position as me where they really don't want to start their real job, quote unquote, or they want a break from their real job." In addition to removing themselves from their current work situations, many long-distance hikers have recently finished high school or college, like Turbo and Kodak, and want a break before starting their careers, so they head to the Appalachian Trail. When walking long distance, hikers find themselves with hours of uninterrupted time, far away from the world of asphalt and traffic lights, in a place where they can think about and resolve issues.

THE MAKING OF LONG-DISTANCE HIKERS/ LONG-DISTANCE HIKERS MAKE THEMSELVES

Long-distance hikers are made, not born. As a result of this chosen lifestyle of poverty that emerges as individuals engage in long-distance hiking, those outside the hiking community "construct" or create images or representations of long-distance hikers that have little to do with hikers' self-perceived realities. Nonetheless, these boundaries allow a long-distance hiker identity and a cohesive group or community to emerge as hikers come to see themselves as "different" from others. This new identity as a long-distance hiker, then, not only reflects how hikers view themselves in comparison to others (particularly nonhikers) but is also a reflection of what hikers do, or the roles and behaviors individuals engage in, as part of the larger hiking community on the Appalachian Trail.

Behind this leisure subculture is a rejection of larger societal structures, both bureaucratic and social, by members of the long-distance hiking community. Many long-distance hikers are no longer motivated by money as they seek refuge in the wilderness away from work or what they consider societal distractions or negatives, such as media influence, consumerism, materialism, stresses of work and family. Long-distance hikers resist structured environments, and the unstructured features associated with long-distance hikers, such as rootlessness, spontaneity, and living outside structured realms of work, production, and property ownership, are invested with positive rather than negative values.

The bodies of long-distance hikers, as well as how hikers interact with and experience their bodies, are also implicated in the construction of a hiker identity. Long-distance hikers are self-disciplined as they continue hiking despite injury or discomfort, unpredictable weather patterns, and difficult terrain. The arduousness of this recreational activity allows long-distance hikers to experience their bodies in unique ways, from the initial hiker's hobble to the evolution of trail legs. To this extent, long-distance hiking is an embodied practice—which is to say that a long-distance hiker identity is created as hikers engage in this extended recreational activity. In many ways, these behaviors, and the relationships that form among long-distance hikers, emerge as a person hikes the Appalachian Trail. They could be considered unique to this place—a topic to which we turn next.

3 ⇥ APRIL'S FOOLS
A Situated Subcultural Identity

April Fool's Day, or April 1, has traditionally been the day long-distance hikers flock in herds to Springer Mountain in Georgia to begin a northbound thru-hike of the Appalachian Trail. For the thousands of individuals who attempt this feat, only about one in four accomplish that goal, with thru-hikers taking anywhere from four to seven months to complete the trail (Appalachian Trail Conservancy 2008). Earl Shaffer is recognized by the Appalachian Trail Conservancy as the first solo thru-hiker. He completed a northbound thru-hike in 1948 and returned again roughly twenty years later to complete a southbound thru-hike. Shaffer, however, was still not finished with the Appalachian Trail. Nearly fifty years after he first began his journey, Shaffer hiked the Appalachian Trail a third time at age seventy-nine, making him the oldest person to complete a thru-hike. He held this honor until 2004, when Lee Barry, aka Easy One, completed the trail at eighty-one years of age.

According to the Appalachian Trail Conservancy, over 12,000 thru-hikers and section hikers have completed the Appalachian Trail to date. Of this number, over 200 have followed in Shaffer's footsteps and have hiked the length of the Appalachian Trail on multiple occasions. This might lead one to wonder exactly what it is about this place, the Appalachian Trail, that brings long-distance hikers like Shaffer and other hikers back time and time again? The answer to this question is explored throughout this chapter.

In the last chapter I outlined many of the key contours of a long-distance hiker identity and argued that because hiking is a physical and social accomplishment, such an identity is formed through both embodied practices and collective bonds. In this chapter I add another critical element to this mix by demonstrating that hiker identities are forged through practices undertaken in a particular setting, namely, the distinctive geography of the Appalachian Trail. In other words, the Appalachian Trail provides long-distance hikers with a unique setting where old identities can be transformed into new ones. Scholars sometimes refer to this process as the formation of "place identity." In what follows, I focus on hikers' singular attachment to the Appalachian Trail. I show how hikers on the AT represent a geographically situated subculture, one that inhabits a place in particular ways and can be identified and understood through a collective and visceral association with territory. There are many culturally distinct traditions associated with the trail, as well as memorable sites along the trail—trail towns, hostels, hiking festivals, shelters—that carry special meaning for long-distance hikers. Long-distance hiking, then, is not only an embodied activity. It is a geographically situated accomplishment that relies heavily on the distinctive environmental and territorial features of the Appalachian Trail.

THE MAKING OF A TRAIL PERSONA

Once on the Appalachian Trail, long-distance hikers take on a new identity, a trail identity, or, according to Sunshine, a twenty-one-year-old section hiker from Connecticut, a "trail persona." But how does this new identity develop? What factors contribute to the emergence of a trail identity for long-distance hikers on the Appalachian Trail? The adoption of a trail name is the first of many cultural traditions hikers engage in that reinforces an attachment to the trail. In fact, the first question long-distance hikers on the Appalachian Trail ask one another at first encounter is, "What is your trail name?" As Lady Mustard Seed explained it, "You know when you meet a thru-hiker as opposed to a weekender because they immediately ask for your name. . . . A weekender doesn't care. They might ask you how the trail is, but a thru-hiker's going to immediately ask you your name."

The Giving and Receiving of Trail Names

The giving and receiving of trail names is a cultural tradition that leads to hikers' increased attachment to the Appalachian Trail, as well as to the hiking community. The following dialogue between married couple Kutsa and

Montreal and myself demonstrates the extent to which a trail name can become an essential part of one's identity as a result of hiking the Appalachian Trail:

KUTSA: This is my identity because in Israel I am Shelly and this is totally my other life. My whole family is there, my friends, but that is my past. And since I started hiking and I became Kutsa, everybody on the trail, [Montreal's] family, friends know that I'm only Kutsa. This is my adventure name. This is my freedom name. There are no ties to this name. There is no bad past. It's only good. It's achieving. It's fun and it's the [Appalachian] Trail. . . . [Montreal] always calls me Kutsa, but if suddenly on the phone my mom calls and he says, "Shelly," I'm like oh, don't say that.

MONTREAL: Yeah, I call her Kutsa. My family knows her as Kutsa.

KUTSA: Yeah, they know me just by Kutsa because it really became me.

For those, like Kutsa, who are fully immersed in the hiking community, birth names are not used and possibly not known to other hikers. Happy Feet, the partially blind thirty-year-old thru-hiker from Texas, discussed the uniqueness of trail names. When asked if he thought trail names added to the trail experience or possibly took away from it, Happy Feet replied, "You don't walk up to somebody on the street and say, 'Hey, Big Head' or whatever so it's a unique characteristic to the AT in itself. If you run into someone who says, 'Hey, I'm Slow Going' or 'Baldy' or something like that you know that they're a hiker."

Trail names are not a unique characteristic of Appalachian Trail thru-hikers. Evidence suggests that hikers on other long-distance trails are also identified by trail names. In my review of online hiking journals by long-distance hikers on the Pacific Crest Trail, I found hikers who had adopted a trail name. After speaking with someone at the Pacific Crest Trail Association in February 2009, however, I learned that the majority of Pacific Crest hikers had previously thru-hiked the Appalachian Trail before attempting the PCT. My hunch is that the adoption of trail names originated on the Appalachian Trail and that the tradition or practice spread as hikers attempted to hike the Triple Crown. Regardless of origin, trail names allow hikers to adopt a new identity (if desired); they provide a rich source of association in an unfamiliar but unique context and convey more about a person than would a name like "Valerie" or "Sean."

For hikers on the AT, trail names are a rite of passage and represent one way long-distance hikers distinguish themselves from others when hiking the Appalachian Trail, as noted earlier by Lady Mustard Seed and Happy Feet. Although more than 90 percent of long-distance hikers on the AT adopt a trail name (Mueser 1998), not everyone participates in this symbolic renaming of themselves or others. The opportunity a hiker has to interact with others in order to be given a name may depend on where he or she starts hiking. The majority of long-distance hikers on the Appalachian Trail are northbounders (NOBOs), meaning they begin in Georgia at Springer Mountain, the southern terminus, and hike north. Southbounders (SOBOs), on the other hand, begin their hike in Maine at Mount Katahdin, the northern terminus, and hike south. When Kodak first began her thru-hike, she told me about a couple of SOBOs she met in Georgia who were finishing their thru-hikes. Naturally, she asked what their trail names were. Kodak soon realized "they hadn't taken trail names because they thought that it was ridiculous, that you didn't represent yourself if you had this façade or other identity." A possible reason trail names were not adopted by the two SOBOs may be because they were not hiking with others and thus did not experience the camaraderie that often emerges among long-distance hikers traveling north.

The adoption of a trail name comes about in one of two ways. Although trail names primarily arise out of interactions with fellow hikers, reflecting how one is seen or experienced by others, some hikers choose a name before starting the trail; often that name is symbolic of their personal reasons for making the journey. Lady Mustard Seed chose her name prior to hiking the trail. She admitted wanting a name that was symbolic of her reasons for hiking. The year before she and her husband decided to hike the Appalachian Trail, Lady Mustard Seed participated in a Bible study based on the book of Mark. She remarked:

> There is a passage in Mark that says, "If you have faith like a mustard seed, say to this mountain move and it will move." Essentially that's what is says. So, a mustard seed is a very, very small thing. It's like a grain of sand and it grows into a huge, huge, huge bush. So, that's where the mustard seed comes in. And I tell people it's really a meditation. I'm trying to conjure up the faith of a mustard seed. I don't want to hike over mountains, I want to move it (laughs). But

I, really, seriously, it's a mediation because I need that faith. I need that faith to get to Maine.

Unlike Lady Mustard Seed, who chose her trail name prior to hiking, Turbo, unbeknownst to him at the time, was given his trail name by two thru-hikers he met his first night on the Appalachian Trail at Gooch Gap Shelter in Georgia. Turbo would not see these two until their paths crossed again in the Smokies. When Turbo caught up to them, the two hikers asked if he had a trail name yet, to which Turbo replied no. The two told him, "we've been calling you Turbo since the day we met you, you know, I wonder what Turbo's up to, where's Turbo, what's he doing?" Laughing, Turbo said, the name "just kind of stuck." Turbo said he really did not do more miles than other hikers, even though that might have appeared to be the case, especially after he was able to take a week off at Nantahala Gorge and still catch them, but "they just say it's my demeanor, the way I go about, especially at camp" that resulted in his trail name. Turbo was not one to linger around at camp in the mornings but would rather make a quick breakfast of "cold instant oatmeal dry" and be on his way.

Trail names also provide a link among fellow hikers and to the trail even after their hiking experience is over. Drifter, the repeat thru-hiker met in chapter 1, offered an example of how trail names reinforce hikers' attachments to the Appalachian Trail:

I've got a lot of friends from years ago who I am still friends with and when we get together real names don't come into play. I mean my buddy Otter, who is my brother until the day one of us dies, he will always be Otter. It doesn't matter what his real name is. I think when you have that, I don't even know what to call it, it's when you're, when we are referring to each other as Otter and Drifter at home we're still sort of in our heads here. It's a way to keep the dream alive so to speak. It's such a big experience to so many people that we don't want to let it go completely and I think that's just a way for us to do it very subtly so we don't bother a lot of people with it (laughs). But it's kind of cool. I have a lot of people in my life who only call me Drifter, and there's a lot of people in my life who I only refer to by their trail names. Whenever we get together it's, regardless of what part of the country or what we're doing, it's always a trail-related feeling, and we always talk about the trail. We always go back to the old experiences on the trail. So, that's, I think that's one thing the trail names allow us. We can keep living that little, that part of our lives.

For Drifter, even the use of trail names quickly takes him back to the trail, reinforcing a trail identity. He also suggested that trail names create a sense of community, connecting hikers with others encountered along their way. Branch explained, "It's definitely the subculture to have a trail name. To have a trail name means you are in the subculture. You automatically feel like you're a part of the community." Kodak said she hiked for three weeks and was the only person in her group without a trail name, which she admits was a little upsetting. While she was with the hiking community, Kodak did not feel she completely belonged until she was given a trail name. Like Branch and Kodak, Phoenix Rising also suggested that trail names provide hikers with a sense of community or family. According to her, trail names are what long-distance hikers share in common and what she believes sets them apart from everyone else, both on and off the trail.

Trail Magic

Trail names, however, are not the only cultural tradition that reinforces hikers' attachments to the Appalachian Trail. There is the phenomenon called trail magic, "known and spoken of with reverence," according to humor and travel writer Bill Bryson, "which holds that often when things look darkest some little piece of serendipity comes along to put you back on a heavenly plane." Trail magic not only reinforces this newly adopted trail identity but also brings hikers together, albeit unexpectedly, to help create community.

Trail magic is both an event and a cultural tradition that long-distance hikers have come to associate with, and even expect to experience on, the Appalachian Trail. More often than not, trail magic comes when least expected but most needed. Trail magic can be many things to different hikers, including, but not limited to, a kind word from a stranger, a ride, the finding of a lost item, or an elaborate spread of food. Regardless of the form it takes, trail magic helps create strong social and emotional attachments to the Appalachian Trail, and it is something that long-distance hikers reflect on fondly.

For most hikers, trail magic has become associated with food and drink. Elaborate spreads of food, increasingly referred to as "trail catering" by some, is one such opportunity that allows long-distance hikers to come together at random times and locations along the trail. Swinging Jane offered an example and described a "complete spread" in which "there was lunch meat of all kinds, pops of all kinds, chips, cheeses, cookies, cakes, and brownies" as well as a second place filled with "hotdogs and slaw and condiments to put on them, and chips." Such trail magic is conferred by trail angels, typically defined as individuals who bestow random acts of kindness on hikers. Trail angels are sometimes anonymous, but often they are former hikers, local religious congregations, and hiking clubs, who return year after year to meet hikers' nutritional needs and show their support through trail magic. For example, some former thru-hikers, who know from experience how long it takes to get from Springer Mountain to Neels Gap, as well as exactly what sort of food hikers might crave at that point in their hike, return as trail angels, setting up in the same place on the trail. Thus, the current year's hikers are not the only ones along the Appalachian Trail who are beginning to adopt a trail identity. Former hikers have such strong attachments to the Appalachian Trail that they come back to provide support and encouragement to the hiking community.

On occasions such as those just described, long-distance hikers are able to sit down and relax, even if only momentarily, before continuing their journey. There may even be occasions when hikers are able to stay overnight. Slick recalled one such experience:

> The best one that I've been to so far was in Addis Gap, which was really early on the trail. It was one of the first two weeks. It was actually in one of the first few days now that I think about it. I think they started April 1 and they were out there for a week and they must have spent hundreds of dollars on food. They had everything. It was out in the woods off some forest road. They had tents, they had kegs in the creek, they had all these huge bottles of Southern Comfort whiskey, they had just everything. They were so nice, "Come on in, stay with us." A lot of people stayed the night there . . . unfortunately, I was sick when we came through there, so I just came in and one of the ladies was like, "Go lay in the hammock and I'll make you a sandwich." She kind of momma'd me for a little while which was really nice because I was feeling really sick. I think that has been the best one.

Examples of trail magic such as Slick describes can be emotional experiences for long-distance hikers. It is this emotional element that allows hikers to become attached to the trail; this is where the trail magic occurs. As Slick points out below, being on the receiving end of trail magic can have a profound influence on a hiker's emotional state:

> Trail magic is something that seems to get you from one spot to another or push through the harder days, because you can be having the worst day and you'll come around the corner and someone's sitting there cooking hotdogs for you. And you're like, oh, my gosh, that's just awesome! You'd think you'd won the lottery. It's nice little treats. It's a little motivational.

Trail magic does not have to be an elaborate spread of food, however. Trail magic can also take the form of a cold six-pack of soda or beer floating in a stream or an army green lockbox full of miniature chocolates located at a random location in the middle of the trail, like the one my hiking partner and I encountered in southern Virginia near McAfee Knob. In these instances the givers of trail magic are simply unknown. It is almost like the trail itself is giving to hikers. Whereas trail magic might be expected, or at the very least anticipated, at road crossings, it is a rare occasion to come across trail magic on the trail, miles from a road crossing, much less high up on a mountain.

Interestingly, the cultural tradition of giving trail magic appears to be more common along the southern portion of the Appalachian Trail. One such surprise my hiking partners and I experienced, left by anonymous trail angels, was at a road crossing in central Virginia. There was a large blue cooler full of flavored sports drinks, root beer, candy bars, potato chips, and fresh fruit with a sign reading "Hikers help yourselves." The timing could not have been more perfect! It was just what we needed before our next big climb.

I am not sure if the occurrence of trail magic in the southern portion of the trail is due to "southern hospitality" or the simple fact that most people begin in Georgia at Springer Mountain and hike north. Of the 2,000 or so who begin their hike in Georgia, about half make it to Damascus for the Trail Days Festival. Roughly 500 make it to Harper's Ferry, the psychological halfway point, and about 250 actually finish their thru-hike at the trail's northern terminus, Mount Katahdin. Hustler, who completed a thru-hike the previous year, also noticed what might be referred to as regional friendliness:

Down south everybody is real friendly. Up north . . . New York, there are some real friendly folks there, but Massachusetts . . . they weren't as friendly in New England. They just thought you were hiker trash or something, I don't know. I mean you look like a complete bum when you come out of the woods. You're not shaven well, you smell, you're wet. They're like, "What's this riff-raff doing in our town?" but down here they are really used to seeing it. By the time you get up there, there's less people. Most of the hikers, 80 percent of the thru-hikers have dropped off by the time you get to New England, and there just aren't that many of us up there and they aren't as used to seeing us. There are [fewer] hostels up there, too, so there's not as many, there's not a support net to help you out as much. But then Maine was real friendly. But the farther north you get it seems as if people aren't as friendly. It's harder to get rides, with Maine being the exception. But down here is real nice.

One possibility that I have thought of, which was vocalized as well by Hustler, is that people in the southern states are used to seeing long-distance hikers and are aware of the Appalachian Trail, whereas those in the northern states may not be. It could also be that churches up north are not as interested in proselytizing in quite the same way that those in the south seem to be, though they may operate a hiker hostel, allowing hikers to stay overnight for a small donation. Regardless of the reason, in my experience and from what other hikers have shared with me, the farther north you hike, the fewer instances of trail magic there are, particularly those elaborate spreads of food.

Though it may seem as if trail magic is equated with food and drink, trail magic also refers to anything a hiker needs most to encourage him or her on the journey. This could be a ride into town, a kind word or smile from a fellow hiker, experiences found in nature, or the return or replacement of a lost piece of equipment. Socks and her husband were hiking in Connecticut when Socks realized she had forgotten her bandana. Naturally they did not want to backtrack to get it. As they continued hiking another quarter of a mile down the trail, Socks's husband said, "Do you still believe in that trail magic stuff?" She looked down to find a bandana lying right in the middle of the trail. Again, this sort of experience gives hikers a feeling of deep association with the trail. In this instance, trail magic was not given by trail angels, but the trail itself fulfilled Socks's need.

Kodak refers to these experiences on the trail as "the other kind of trail magic." She described the day she hiked up McAfee Knob and the Tinker Cliffs. The fog was thick, and she did not get to see one of the most photographed scenic outlooks on the trail, McAfee Knob, and she was feeling a little down. As she continued the climb, she noticed there were "these little salamanders and they were bright orange and they made my day right there."

I can relate to both Socks and Kodak. At one point I was having difficulty staying motivated and just wanted to quit my hike and go home. Sweat was pouring off of me as I walked alone, climbing what seemed like a mountain that had no summit. I had not had a shower or meal other than dehydrated noodles and cold oatmeal for probably a week. I was literally near tears. Right about then, I glanced to my left and saw a flowering plant, lily of the valley to be exact. At that moment I knew I was not alone out there. I could feel myself almost being carried up the rest of the mountain, as the hymn "The Lily of the Valley" played over and over in my head. At this point, my whole demeanor changed and a smile began to form as I continued up the mountain. Whereas trail magic in the form of "hiker feeds" strengthens camaraderie among the hiking community, it is this type of trail magic, magic found through hiking the trail itself, that creates strong attachments to the physical geography of the trail, reinforcing a trail identity.

Trail magic also occurs when someone invites you into their home for the night. Hatchet Jack described such an experience:

> There was this sign that said trail magic, go down to the road, take a right, it will be worth your walk. And we go up there and the people take us into their house. They give us a three-course meal. They give us Belgian waffles with syrup and then they give us a barbeque sandwich, potato salad, Jell-O. Then they give us a dessert and they had like four different kinds of dessert to choose from. And then they have all these books and we could just take any books we wanted to read. It was just really nice. It's just amazing that someone can take a dirty hiker into their nice house and share everything they have.

Hatchet Jack's story suggests that those outside the immediate hiking community on the Appalachian Trail also play a role in the construction of a trail identity for long-distance hikers. In other words, experiences like those Hatchet Jack describes make hiking the Appalachian Trail a special, memorable experience. When interacting with nonhikers, Hatchet Jack is now aware of whom he has become—"a dirty hiker"—an identity he and others have come to associate with the trail. So, not only does the cultural tradition of trail magic contribute to the making of a trail identity. Leaving the Appalachian Trail for a short time has the potential to reinforce this newly adopted trail identity. As such, migration on and off the trail becomes a foundational event in the making of a trail identity for long-distance hikers.

Migration: A Foundational Event

For many hikers, traveling through local communities, as the Appalachian Trail does at times, or leaving the trail completely to resupply in a town, stay overnight, or return home, reinforces a deep attachment to and longing for the trail. While at Trail Days in Damascus, Virginia, I spoke with Taz about her experiences in local communities. Specifically, I was curious if she ever looked forward to leaving town to return to the trail. After a short pause Taz replied, "You get an itch. You just get a feeling that you need to get back out on the trail really soon." I then asked if staying longer in town, like for Trail Days, made it more difficult to go back to the trail. Taz thoughtfully replied:

It probably is that way. I've been in town for a week now but I'm leaving tomorrow. I've already gotten my stuff ready and everything is organized and planned. But I'm pretty sure. Sometimes it's just a day, sometimes it's two days, but you just get the feeling that you've got to get on the move again. I can't explain it and I don't know where it comes from either. I just think the trail becomes you.

Taz is not the only hiker who recognized this transformation occurring within herself. Sitting around a shelter after dinner, Drifter described a similar feeling, saying, flatly, "Being on the trail changes people." When I asked him to elaborate, Drifter explained:

There is just something that I think is really cool out here and I didn't know it would happen and it happened in 1994. It's like this change you go through, like a metamorphosis where at some point in the hike you're more comfortable in the woods than you are in the towns. You'd much rather do the hit-and-run get what you need in the town and get back out onto the AT with your friends as fast as you can. I think it happens at a different point in the hike for everybody. It hasn't totally happened for me yet this year, but I know plenty of people who are already much more comfortable out here.

In this way, Drifter echoes Taz's statement that "the trail becomes you." To be sure, the practice of long-distance hiking is a transformative feat. It is not, however, just a physical accomplishment. And it is certainly not undertaken in neutral space. Long-distance hiking is altogether different than, say, walking on a treadmill day after day. Gradually a hiker's place identity emerges—or is cultivated—such that a personal attachment to the physical territory of the Appalachian Trail becomes stronger the more time a hiker spends on the trail. Drifter also acknowledges, however, that this "metamorphosis . . . happens at a different point in the hike for everybody."

For Pebble, the change happened fairly quickly. Pebble had hiked fifty miles on the Appalachian Trail as part of a college class at Christopher Newport University before she attempted a thru-hike the following year. She was more than willing to discuss both events with me:

> I actually went home Sunday and stayed last week and slackpacked. It was very different. From the class I had more of a shock. My apartment was small when I went back from the class. Very confining. I would go up to the roof for a view. That really bugged me. The bathroom. Having one spot to have to go to the bathroom where if I was somewhere else and I needed to go and I was in the woods I could just go. Having to go somewhere, that was really weird. When I went back just recently it was different to have clothes. I had my makeup on. It was so weird. I think all I did was eyeliner and it felt immensely different. Clothes. I don't feel normal anymore. I couldn't wait to get back into my hiking clothes once they were clean. Being around my parents was really different, too. It wasn't the hiker community I was used to.

Pebble admitted feeling confined to her apartment when she went home from her class experience. She had become accustomed to being in an open environment where she was not relegated to "rooms" for various reasons or confronting walls that blocked her view of the outside. Although only on the Appalachian Trail for a short period (a couple of weeks for the class), Pebble's attachment to the trail was significant enough and her trail identity strong enough to make her uncomfortable in her college

apartment. I myself found it difficult to sleep inside on a bed upon returning home and a few times pitched my tent in the backyard just to feel "normal" again.

Unlike the two-week stint hiking with her college class, Pebble started
her thru-hike in Georgia at the southern terminus and, when I talked
with her, had been hiking with others for 473 miles. As a result of her
previous experience, she had already adopted a trail identity. When she
went home for the week and slackpacked, she noticed how different the
experience was both in terms of her sense of self and as part of a community.
In other words, Pebble had not only developed an identity in relation to the
Appalachian Trail but now considered herself part of the hiking community as well. (Slackpacking most often occurs when hikers want to make big
miles without the weight of a heavy pack to slow them down. Essentially,
hikers will take a small day pack with a little food and water and leave their
big pack behind with someone who drops them off and then picks them up
at the end of the day.)

Most of my interactions with long-distance hikers occurred during their
hike, and I did not have any opportunities to speak with hikers after they
returned home. Drifter, however, mentioned that he had thru-hiked the
Appalachian Trail on two previous occasions, the first in 1994, so I inquired
about what it was like to return home after spending four to seven months
hiking in the woods. Drifter took a deep breath and replied:

> You give yourself some time back home where you still control your struc-
> tured daily routine. In other words, if you can take a month after your hike
> before you go back to work, good, because that will sort of smooth out the
> reentry process. Otherwise, it's like breaking through the atmosphere. All
> of a sudden you're just on fire and you can't control anything. Reentry, the
> first time . . . I just freaked out getting back into the environment that I was
> in. I lasted about five months in my job before I quit it and I spent the next
> two years living in a tent working as a whitewater rafting guide in Kentucky
> because I just couldn't handle getting back into a normal routine. It didn't
> work for me. I learned enough out here to know that what I was doing before
> wasn't going to be working for me. It took me five months of getting back into
> it to figure that out. But reentry is not something, again, that I look forward to
> or that I would wish upon anybody. It can be real hard, but it doesn't bother
> some people at all.

Drifter continued to suggest that for hikers who have been on the trail for an extended period of time, "the transition is often full of intense emotion." Drifter also acknowledged that others do not have trouble adjusting at all, despite the initial shock. Still other hikers, such as Gus, a sixty-two-year-old section hiker from Massachusetts, get nervous at the thought of going home and do have difficulty adjusting to life after the trail.

Kutsa shared that, for her, a deep depression sets in after leaving the trail. Kutsa first heard of the Appalachian Trail in 1999 when she read an article about the first Israeli woman to complete a thru-hike. Kutsa, herself from a tiny village in Israel of approximately eighty families, thought a long-distance hike sounded "really cool" and made the decision two months later to try it herself. She hiked about 1,200 miles on the AT in 2000, 400 miles in 2001, and thru-hiked the entire trail in 2002, when she met Montreal, who is now her husband. Kutsa strongly believed that she had finally found her passion on the Appalachian Trail and continues to search for something to do when she is not hiking. She added that she did not have much outside of the trail because the Appalachian Trail was her life.

For hikers like Kutsa, their trail identity or persona becomes so strong that it remains a part of who they are when they are no longer on the trail. I often wondered what hikers took away from their trail experience or learned about themselves as a result of this unique experience. Once again, Drifter was more than happy to share as he reflected on his 1994 thru-hike:

Well, I learned, probably just like anybody who would complete an experience like this, that we are able to handle a lot more than we think we can. It definitely served to (laughs) kind of strengthen my faith in people. I was pretty cynical. I was a lot different of a person then than I am now. People are basically good and I look at people a lot differently now than I did eleven years ago and that is just one of probably a lot of things that I've hung onto over these years and will probably hang onto for the rest of my life. . . . Because like I said, I was a pretty tough case coming out here in 1994. I was very cynical and wasn't happy, and this whole experience calmed me down and made me realize that it ain't so bad after all. It's all how you make it. And I carry that with me on a daily basis just like I do so many other experiences on the trail. You never, if you do a hike like this, you never, I don't think you ever lose it. If it was really a meaningful experience to you, I don't think you ever lose it. You have, to this day I still have flashbacks at

home of places I've been, the things that I have done, and just for no reason. You'll be in the middle of doing something at home and bam, you're
on a mountaintop in Maine or wherever, just these wonderful images and
moments come back to you. That's like one of the greatest things and I
don't think I'll ever lose that and I don't think anybody who does this will
ever lose that. It's a benefit that you didn't know you were going to get and
it's a great part of the trip.

As Drifter suggests, the physical activity of long-distance hiking, along with
the extended period of time engaging with the Appalachian Trail, often
leaves hikers feeling "different," leading to a change in lifestyle once hikers
return home. Clearly, Drifter carries his trail experiences with him on a daily
basis and admits these experiences have changed him and become a part of
who he is today. This new identity, as well as his experiences on the trail, is
part of what compels Drifter to return to the Appalachian Trail time and
again, as it does for so many other hikers. To be sure, Pebble, Drifter, and
Kutsa were not the only hikers who talked about the difficulty of switch-
ing from their newly adopted trail identity or trail life to the "real world," as
hikers commonly refer to life off the trail. Once they leave the Appalachian
Trail and return home, many long-distance hikers are confronted with a loss
of identity and community.

Though migration on and off the Appalachian Trail is a foundational
event for long-distance hikers and contributes to a trail identity, subcultures
also create their own geography, or a set of sites or places, through which
members gain cohesion and identity. In other words, several memorable
sites unique to the Appalachian Trail also play a part in the making of a
trail identity and, subsequently, the creation of a geographically situated
subculture.

Creating Their Own Geography

There are many designated campsites, shelters, and hostels, and various pre-
planned events along or near the trail that provide long-distance hikers with
the opportunity to interact with each other. In fact, these places are the only
established social centers that bring hikers together, even if only for a short
time. A majority of shelters are simply three-wall lean-tos made of wood
(see fig. 5), sometimes stone (see fig. 6), placed roughly eight to ten miles
apart, although the distance between them varies. At most shelters, there is

5. Swansong Shelter, built on private land, is a "secret shelter" on the Appalachian Trail south of Killington, Vermont, 2010. This shelter is not listed in any guidebooks and can only be found by hikers if they know where to look. Photograph by author.

a water source and tent sites for camping, although tent sites are not always an option due to the location or terrain.

Trail shelters may seem to be fairly generic structures, but each has a unique name or personality, for example: Blood Mountain, Thomas Knob, where feral ponies come to visit (see fig. 7), Raccoon Branch, Punchbowl (said to be haunted by four-year-old Ottie Cline Powell, who died in 1891 when he left a schoolhouse to hunt for firewood with his brothers), Lost Mountain, No Business Knob, Standing Indian, Wawayanda, War Spur, Trimpi (with stone fireplace), Eagles Nest, Moxie Bald, and The Priest (a true confessional), to name a few. And then there is Partnership Shelter, one of the more well-known shelters on the Appalachian Trail (see fig. 8). Hikers refer to this shelter, located a quarter of a mile from the Mount Rogers Visitor Center, as the Taj Mahal of shelters on the Appalachian Trail. Everyone I met could not wait to get to Partnership for the solar shower and pizza. Yes, pizza! Because of its proximity to the visitor center, pizza can

6. Hikers packing up and getting ready to start the day at Happy Hill Shelter, a stone shelter just south of the Vermont–New Hampshire border, 2010. Photograph by author.

be delivered. Every day, a new group of hikers comes together and orders pizza, feasting upon the many toppings and combinations at Partnership for the remainder of the day and often well into the evening.

Pizza and water are not the only reasons hikers find themselves drawn to the shelters on the Appalachian Trail. Since many hikers spend most of the day hiking alone, they may choose to spend the night in shelters, which hiker T-Mac describes as "social outposts . . . in the middle of the woods." Hustler admits to being "a shelter rat" for this very reason, stating he gets "lonely after a while." And though Rez Dog does not typically stay over- night in the shelters, he also makes it a point to at least stop by the shelters simply because he really enjoys seeing the people there. He admitted that the social interaction, meeting people, was good for him.

Gus likes to stay in shelters both because he does not like to carry the extra weight of a tent and because he appreciates the social aspects. He remarked, "You hope that everybody that comes in is kind of a nice person"

7. On an extremely cold day, a lone hiker prepares to cook dinner at Thomas Knob Shelter in southern Virginia while feral ponies graze nearby, 2011. Photograph by author.

so you can visit and "talk about your experience on the trail" before turning in for the night. But, as Montreal indicated, trail experiences are not all that may be shared:

> You will see a lot of people in shelters. I had great discussions with people I met only one time. Some older people, some younger, and the sun was going down and you are talking and talking until everything becomes dark and you continue talking and people open themselves and tell you stuff that they wouldn't even say to their best friends because they won't see you necessarily, because you shared something very deep. They have all these emotions coming out because it's the right place at the right time. The right experiences. It's something very new for them and it's very interesting just to share these experiences. I think this is part of the journey. You won't necessarily remember everything but it just adds to your life backpack, you know?

8. A large gathering of hikers, excited about the solar shower and pizza, at Partnership Shelter in 2005. Photograph courtesy of Christopher W. Bounds.

Clearly shelters dotting the Appalachian Trail provide hikers with the opportunity to come together, even if only briefly, and are a unique aspect of the trail experience. But shelters are not the only social centers or memorable sites for hikers on the Appalachian Trail. Bear's Den Rocks in Virginia, a stone lodge built by local stonemasons in 1933 turned hiker hostel, is located in the middle of the twenty-mile "Roller Coaster" section of the Appalachian Trail and is a popular overnight stop for long-distance hikers wanting a shower, bed, pizza, and pint of Ben and Jerry's ice cream.

Speaking of ice cream, Pine Grove Furnace State Park, in Pennsylvania, is home to a well-known cultural tradition that brings hikers together at the Pine Grove Furnace Store. Long before reaching this area in south central Pennsylvania, near the official halfway point of the Appalachian Trail, I heard tales of the Half Gallon Challenge. The Half Gallon Challenge is a long-distance hiker tradition, and anyone hiking from Maine or Georgia who makes it this far has the opportunity to join the Half Gallon Club. The challenge, after purchasing a half gallon of ice cream, is to eat it as quickly as possible. Although as a section hiker I could have participated in the challenge, I chose not to do so—partly because I did not feel I had earned it and partly because of the misery that may follow. While my hiking partner and I were with Bonzo in Harper's Ferry, he inquired as to whether we planned on participating in the Half Gallon Challenge. His only advice: "Be sure you have lots of toilet paper for later!"

The day we made it to the Pine Grove Furnace Store, we met two thru-hikers who were going to attempt the challenge while we were there. I can report that they met the challenge head on, and both young men became members of the Half Gallon Club. We enjoyed their company, and the four of us shared a campsite at Pine Grove Furnace State Park that night. We spent a few hours telling stories about our trail experiences around the campfire and talking about other hikers we had met along the way. Eventually one of the men, T-Mac, told us that Turbo, the other guy, had paid dearly for his ice cream indulgence by, among other things, not making it to the bathhouse in time. Needless to say, my hiking partner and I were satisfied that we had opted out of this Appalachian Trail tradition.

Another well-known hostel on the trail is Wood's Hole near Pearisburg, Virginia. This particular hostel, which provides hikers with an opportunity to work together communally, was previously owned by Miss Tillie, who had been opening her doors to hikers since 1986. Every morning throughout the summer, she made homemade biscuits, sausage, eggs, and coffee for the early risers, for a small donation, of course. I was fortunate to stay there in 2005 and feast on her homemade biscuits. Since Miss Tillie's death in 2008, her granddaughter Neville and husband, who met during his 2005 thru-hike, now run the hostel. While the spirit and love that fill the small cabin still remain, Wood's Hole has changed in some ways. When I visited in 2012, and more recently in 2014, the biggest change was a shift to sustainable living practices that included beekeeping, vermaculture or worm wrangling, a vegetable garden, farm animals, including pigs, goats, chickens, and pheasants, and installation of an outdoor furnace that has greatly reduced their electric bill. Breakfast and dinner are still offered to hikers passing through for a small fee. While there, all hikers assist with preparation of the meal and cleanup. These shared experiences, as well as cultural traditions like the Half Gallon Challenge, trail magic, and the giving and receiving of trail names, all help create community and reinforce a trail identity for long-distance hikers on the Appalachian Trail.

In addition to memorable sites and cultural traditions, there are pre-planned events and festivals along the route throughout the summer and fall, such as Trailfest in Hot Springs, North Carolina, and Trails End Festival in Millinocket, Maine, each year. They too reinforce hikers' attachment to the trail, as well as to the hiking community. One of the largest gatherings of long-distance hikers, if not the largest, transpires every May in Damascus, Virginia, at Trail Days. Hobo Joe, a twenty-year-old thru-hiker from Massachusetts, offered an explanation as to why Trail Days was the highest point of the hike for him:

> It was just this huge sense of community and huge sense of, kind of like once you're out here you really belong to this group of people. It's very exclusive in the way, that unless you know about it from being on the trail, you wouldn't necessarily know that it even existed. It was one of the most memorable experiences for me, especially community-wise. Just to know that there are so many people out here that will never forget their hike and will always remember and always come back to relive memories and all that.

For many long-distance hikers, Trail Days is similar to a high school class reunion. Festival events include a hiker talent show as well as a parade. For the hiker parade, held on the Saturday of the festival, long-distance hikers come together and make a banner for their hiking class, which they carry in front of them as they hike through the town of Damascus. As may be recalled from chapter 1, the highlight of the parade is the water fight between long-distance hikers, past and present, and the local townspeople and visitors. Lady Mustard Seed described the event while laughing and smiling the entire time:

> Well, the balloon fight (laughs) . . . I don't even know what to say (smiles). It was the rowdiest thing I've ever been in the middle of . . . it was crazy! You're in the middle of just this mob of hikers and everyone has water balloons and water guns and I only had my Nalgene. It was pouring down rain. It was raining so hard that the poor little high school band could not march. They got cancelled. And we were just walking down the street. The locals, in the beginning, there's houses on either side where the people that live there in the community are just watching the hikers go by. And they were attacked by the hikers, and throwing balloons at the hikers, and the hikers were

throwing balloons at them. And if people saw it . . . there were guys with huge water guns and they saw locals standing in their yard and they just ran up and fought with them. I just laughed the whole way. It was such a retreat to childhood. Yes! I just laughed and laughed and laughed. It was so much fun!

As described by Hobo Joe and Lady Mustard Seed, events like Trail Days in Damascus, "the friendliest town on the AT," create cohesion and solidarity among the hiking community as hikers, new and old, come together to share and relive their trail experiences.

Many long-distance hikers find that their most memorable trail experiences are related to the social aspects of the trail. Perhaps Señor Nobs, a thirty-four-year-old return thru-hiker from Minnesota, said it best: "There's not a single story. It has to do with people. It's always about the people. When I take out my pictures and review my trail experience from last time it's a picture of the people that I remember."

Clearly, the Appalachian Trail provides hikers ample opportunity for social interaction, and this trail has an international reputation for doing just that. Gypsy Lulu, a twenty-three-year-old thru-hiker from Michigan, acknowledged that "there are many gorgeous trails all over the world." She was drawn to the Appalachian Trail, as was Turbo, because of "all the different people that you meet and all the people that live on the trail who love to help out, the camaraderie and stuff." The social aspect is part of the reason people come back year after year. It's like coming home to family.

A Geographically Situated Subculture

Bonzo, my friend from Harper's Ferry, playfully suggested that if he were the only hiker out there on the Appalachian Trail, he'd trip himself "and wish for death." He frequently referred to the hiking community as family, which is one reason he enjoys providing trail magic to other hikers by inviting them into his home:

> The hiking community is kind of like family to me. I'm close to it. I like the people that are out there and normally the people that make it here, whether they are hiking south or north, are serious about it. A lot of the riff-raff is gone. And it's just like family. I wouldn't go five miles anywhere around here and meet a total stranger and invite them back here. I just wouldn't. I wouldn't do it. But hikers? You smell like butt, you're coming to my place.

As indicated earlier, many long-distance hikers admit that the social aspect is half of their trail experience. Boone, a thru-hiker in his early twenties from North Carolina, chose to thru-hike the Appalachian Trail because, in his own words, "It's kind of the really classic trail." He also added, "It's also the easiest or the safest in another sense [because] there are other people around." Gus also reported feeling "safer out here [on the trail]" than back where he lived. When I asked why he felt there was rarely an occasion to distrust a fellow hiker, Gus replied, "You know, it's a strange phenomenon, but the people out here are just so laid back that you just trust them. You don't fear anybody." This is an interesting statement given that, for the most part, hikers are total strangers to each other. Also, when on the Appalachian Trail, hikers have the opportunity to take on a new identity if desired and become anyone they wish to be. So where does this unconditional trust come from? Clay, an ordained minister and section hiker from Georgia, offered one possible explanation: "The tight-knit community. It's a subculture unlike out in society where one waves to their neighbor through their car window or waves to each other when mowing their lawn. There is definitely, you're sleeping next to a person that you don't know. There's accountability. It's sort of like a primal culture in a sense with modern gear."

As noted by both Gus and Clay, in this new environment long-distance hikers find themselves placing an unreasonable amount of trust in strangers, and this is true both on and off the trail. HeartFire too expressed feeling comfortable on the trail, but she mentioned a concern shared by some female hikers: "women worry about the rape issue, but it's probably closer to town. The thing is not to be near road crossings on the weekends. But in the woods, I feel safe. I feel fine." If long-distance hikers fear anyone, they tend to be cautious of people at road crossings, as HeartFire indicated. They simply do not fear fellow hikers encountered daily on the trail, whether the hiker is someone they know or not. The hiking community watches out for one another.

Living in mainstream society, we are taught to be wary of strangers, which is the complete opposite of the philosophy of long-distance hikers on the Appalachian Trail. T-Mac, whose identity "back home" is that of a Virginia police officer, explained that people want to trust one another on the trail because "everybody's got the same mentality that we're all in this together. We've got a long way to go. We should help each other out and make it a little more enjoyable. . . . Back in the cities, I don't know, you just raise your guard up because back in the city you don't want to open up. You've got to question when people open up or offer you something. You wonder why they are asking." So, as T-Mac suggested, there is something about being on the Appalachian Trail, sharing in the same experiences, that leads hikers to place trust in strangers. Perhaps this is the account-ability that Clay was referring to earlier.

Phoenix Rising offers an example to help understand why hikers place unreasonable amounts of trust in fellow hikers who may be total strangers by referencing the Good Samaritan Bible story:

> I think with thru-hikers you'll see somebody who is much more willing to do something for somebody else. It kind of goes back to the fact that if I'd fallen and a tree was squishing me that somebody I knew would come along and help me first thing. There would be no walking by going "Oh, I don't know." I guess it goes back to the whole Good Samaritan Bible story and who's going to be the one that actually stops. I don't see the general public stopping to help the way they do out here on the trail. You hear stories of people, just walking into the shelter tonight one of the guys said, "Yeah, she saved my life because she was in the shelter and shared her food with me that night. I was running out and it was in the middle of a snowstorm and it was in the Smokies and if it hadn't been for her I may not have made it out of the Smokies." You hear that so often. . . . You don't see that in the normal world, the normal American soci-ety, and that to me is an awesome, awesome thing.

Phoenix Rising focuses on the helpfulness of fellow thru-hikers in their rela-tionships with one another. Compared to "normal" populations, in which expectations are often tied to relationships, long-distance hikers interact and form relationships quite differently. I recall one hiker saying that if someone comes out here to "take" from the trail, or "expect[s]" others to do things for you—as in expectations associated with trail magic, such as food or rides to town—then he or she is missing the point. People should leave the trail with a feeling of wanting to give back to and help others. That is what the Appalachian Trail has to offer those who are willing to listen and respond.

In addition to the trust they place in one another, long-distance hikers also place a great deal of trust in nonhikers, as best illustrated through the cultural tradition of hitchhiking, which occurs on a fairly regular basis along the Appalachian Trail. Boone admitted to accepting rides from people, often without any thought or concern whatsoever. He said people would stop along the side of the highway and say, "You can just leave your bag in the car, I'll meet you at the so and so." He acknowledged that this behavior might suggest he is "an idiot" but defended his behavior by saying they seemed like "really nice people."

Turbo also accepted rides from strangers while hiking the Appalachian Trail but acknowledged that if he were home he would never accept such a ride. He could tell by the look on my face that he needed to explain a little more, so he continued: "It's a different thing unless you want to walk ten miles to town." Turbo and T-Mac defended their behavior by admitting it would be different if they lived near the Appalachian Trail and a guy with a backpack needed a ride. The backpack signifies to them that "the guy's a nice guy" and they would gladly help him. They laughed and playfully added, "He just needs a shower or a hamburger." Back home, if they see a guy with a backpack nowhere near the Appalachian Trail, ninety-nine times out of a hundred they said they would keep going. This exchange with T-Mac and Turbo illustrates the uniqueness of this environment, the Appalachian Trail, when it comes to accepting or offering rides to strangers. Through these interactions and the cultural tradition of hitchhiking, hikers' attachments to the trail become strengthened.

While hikers trust nonhikers, nonhikers also place a significant amount of trust in hikers by inviting them into their vehicles, their homes, or their places of worship. For example, hostels are commonly operated by religious organizations, which invite hikers to stay on the grounds for a small donation. All of these examples indicate there is a reciprocal relationship between hikers and nonhikers (often referred to as trail angels) regarding trust. Turbo recounted one of his more memorable experiences on the trail, which took place in Virginia at Bear's Den Rocks:

> There was a sign that said thru-hikers go around back. So you go around the back and there was this keypad combination deadbolt, and it says use your handbook. The combination is the mileage from someplace to someplace, and so you get all excited and punch in the numbers. It worked, it worked! And you go in and there's a free computer set up with Internet access for hikers, and a phone with free long-distance. It's like, if you're a hiker we trust you not to take our computer. If you're a hiker we trust you not to tear up

our stuff and put graffiti on our beds. It's like if you're a thru-hiker we trust you; come on in.

As Turbo described, Queen Diva, caretaker of the hostel, caters to and trusts long-distance hikers to take care of themselves and the property. Interactions such as these among fellow hikers, and between hikers and nonhikers, play a role in the making of a trail identity and strengthen hikers' attachment to the Appalachian Trail, as well as to the hiking community.

THE RETURN OF APRIL'S FOOLS

The Appalachian Trail becomes a special place for those who have the time, energy, and motivation to make the journey, whether their journey is a few weeks or several months. In fact, many hikers told me that if hikers leave the trail without a feeling of wanting to "give back" to others, to the hiking community specifically and to others more generally, then they have missed the whole point and the gift the Appalachian Trail has to offer. What they mean by this is that the AT gives hikers unique experiences that are then shared among members of this distinct hiking community, or geographically situated subculture. Hikers often speak about the "giving nature of the trail." For many who make the journey, hiking the Appalachian Trail is transformative in that it restores their faith in the goodness of humanity.

So, I ask again, what is it about this place, the Appalachian Trail, that resonates with long-distance hikers, bringing them back time and again? Many come back to bestow trail magic on the current year's hikers, while others come back to relive their experiences and renew friendships, as well as to make new ones. For many, the Appalachian Trail is also a sacred place, a trail to which they become attached socially and emotionally, whether it is the people, the memorable sites or festivals, or the physical geography of the trail itself. Though they acknowledge that there are numerous long-distance hiking trails around the world, many long-distance hikers suggest that the Appalachian Trail has a restorative quality to it. The transformative or healing property hikers have come to associate with the AT is discussed next as I explore the spiritual character of long-distance hiking.

4 ❧ IN SEARCH OF ITHAKA

Long-Distance Hiking
as Spiritual Quest

For Lady Mustard Seed and her husband, North Florida Swamp Donkey, the week leading up to the beginning of their attempt to thru-hike the Appalachian Trail was stressful. They were not yet convinced they would be able to make it "out there" and began to have doubts. Admittedly, the weather was not helping matters one bit. With her mom driving, they arrived at the approach trail to Springer Mountain in the "dripping rain." There was no visibility as the mountain fog was thick and heavy. Lady Mustard Seed recalled this day vividly:

I remember before we left Ben [Swamp Donkey] pouring, trying to pour fuel into our fuel bottle in the parking lot and he spilled it everywhere. My mom, who never said anything about this trip the whole time, finally said, "This is just crazy. That's all I'm going to say about it. I can tell your grandfather I tried to talk you out of it. This is just crazy!" So, off we go. We're just full of nerves. Mom has said her piece, and we take off on the trail. We hadn't been gone eight minutes. Couldn't see anything ahead of us and all of a sudden we see a form kind of appear coming, stepping out of the fog. You could see a leg, then a wooden walking stick, and then white hair and a white beard and this man just appears out of the fog. He says, "Oh, going to Maine, are you?" And we said, "Yes, yes we are." He said, "Oh good for you, you're going to have so much fun." That whole [pause] . . . Ben and I walked a little bit and just looked at each other and said, "Whoa." That was an angel at that moment because that was exactly what . . . we were sooo nervous. We were just so uncomfortable in our own skin. We didn't know if we could do this, and oh, it was tremendous. And that whole day, just being in that fog and going out on a pilgrimage, I just felt like God was telling us this reality is not like reality that you're used to. This trail time is not like any other time. And trail reality is not like home reality. The rules are different out here. And it just seemed that every . . . it just seemed so enchanted. Every tree, every rock, the path itself, I just felt God's benevolence in all of it . . . just embracing us and telling us, "It's going to be okay. Just try. Keep trying."

This scene as described by Lady Mustard Seed sounds as though it could have been taken directly from Washington Irving's *The Legend of Sleepy Hollow*, which depicts a place full of "local tales, haunted spirits, and twilight superstitions" (Irving 2008). Up to this point in their hike, their first day on the Appalachian Trail was by far Lady Mustard Seed's most memorable experience, especially given how nervous and unprepared she and her husband had felt. She continued to talk about their reasons for hiking the trail and explained, "It's just a journey of the self and of the spirit and a journey toward God, that's why we're here." In fact, in the previous passage, Lady Mustard specifically refers to their spiritual journey as a pilgrimage, which to be honest is an accurate comparison. Both long-distance hiking and religious pilgrimage are personal acts of walking a great distance that ends with reaching a final, climatic goal; for the majority of hikers on the Appalachian Trail, the goal is reaching the northern terminus, Maine's Mount Katahdin. Additionally, both hikers and pilgrims may stay in hostels along the way and are often celebrated by those they meet, who help and encourage them on their journey.

In the previous chapter, I charted the development of a trail identity for long-distance hikers as they hike along the Appalachian Trail. I argued that hikers not only develop a trail identity but also come together to create a geographically situated subculture. Because many who hike the trail find themselves at a crossroads or transitional stage in life, the AT becomes a place where many go looking for answers or for meaning in their lives. Consequently, long-distance hikers come to view the Appalachian Trail as a sacred place. In many ways, the Appalachian Trail is a forum for the interweaving of implicit (generically spiritual) and explicit (formal, institutionalized) expressions of religion. This chapter adds another dimension to our understanding of the hiking community by exploring the relationship between long-distance hiking and religious pilgrimage. In what follows, I focus on the three stages of religious pilgrimage as they apply to hikers' experiences: separation from society and life as they know it, a liminal stage where transition takes place, and a reintroduction back into society (Turner 1974). Long-distance hiking, then, is not simply an extended recreational or physical activity. It is a spiritual quest or journey for those who may be lost or for those seeking answers in the solace of the wilderness they hope to find on the Appalachian Trail.

RITES OF SEPARATION

In the first stage of their journey, long-distance hikers find themselves breaking with the practices and routines of their previous lives, whether these had to do with a job, school, or relationships with significant others. Graceful suggested that people get "caught up in the 'real' world and los[e] touch." She also noted that people "are not exactly in the best situation maybe, family situations, maybe drugs, maybe losing jobs, and just searching for something more in their life" and find themselves on the Appalachian Trail. From what I have been told by hikers, some are drawn to the trail because they have experienced the death of a parent or loved one, have recently divorced, have recently finished school or retired from their jobs, or face addictions, as previously noted by Graceful. Regardless of their reasons, during this time hikers experience a metaphorical death, as they leave their former selves and lives behind to hike the Appalachian Trail. Or, as Rez Dog understood it: "I was being driven into exile."

Modern-Day Pilgrims

The practice of long-distance hiking demands that hikers remove themselves from the working world and the multiple roles or identities they occupy in society and spend time on the trail, which gives them a chance to sort through their lives. In chapter 2, Happy Feet mentioned the "corporate yucky" his work environment had become. After searching for something meaningful to do with this life and reading about the Appalachian Trail,

Happy Feet knew this was "the radical change" in his environment that he needed:

> My main goal is not necessarily a goal is to get to Katahdin, but my main goal for this is basically just to have a lot of time available to me away from the world or what I was accustomed to, to basically spend some time working on me and getting back to basics and getting back to the core of who I am. It's praying and spending time with God and just really focusing on, you know, what the next section of my life needs to be and allowing God to work in my life during that. Because if you're too busy worrying about your job or your stresses of life and things like that you have trouble hearing what God has to say to you. So it's best to be silent so that God can speak to you. . . . If I end up going through a particular trail town and God says, "Hey, this is where I need you to be. This is where I need you to stay," then that's the direction that I'm going to take. Like I said, it would be nice to go all the way to Katahdin and things like that but I'm not focused on that. I'm just focused on where God is going to connect me next. And if that takes six months or a year or tomorrow, then fine.

What Happy Feet has described is a modern-day pilgrimage or spiritual journey similar to what Lady Mustard Seed also described. Happy Feet said "a goal" for him was to finish at Mount Katahdin, though at the same time he was motivated for spiritual reasons: he conceived of his main goal as having the quiet time to listen to God. Sure, he acknowledged that there were other situations that would allow God to connect him to other people and to bless other people; however, this self-described "city boy" chose to hike the Appalachian Trail because he believed this new adventure would be an experience that required his faith in God to be the primary director.

Many long-distance hikers on the Appalachian Trail, like Happy Feet and Lady Mustard Seed, are spiritually motivated in their endeavor, unlike most people in mainstream society, whose decision making tends to be financially motivated. Although financial support is necessary for hiking long-distance, many hikers viewed money and possessions as unnecessary distractions. Lady Mustard Seed, for instance, said that hiking the Appalachian Trail spoke to the core of her being, that there was "something very biblical about it—going into the wilderness to wrestle with all that you are and all of those hard parts of yourself . . . to commune with nature and God" so that she might find herself. She said she did not believe she chose to hike the AT of her own free will but that the trail chose her. She explained: "Something of the indwelling spirit, the indwelling Christ in me that told me, 'Come out into the wilderness and find yourself and find Me.'"

Graceful also noted that her ultimate reason for hiking was "to get closer to God," although she did have other reasons for hiking the Appalachian Trail. She further mentioned that there were "a lot of people out here seeking a spiritual, close-to-nature thing." Montreal offered a unique perspective on what hikers may discover or experience once they break from society for the Appalachian Trail:

> I told you about the Zen philosophy. It's always the same thing. You read philosophers who wrote stuff 2,500 years ago and they all say the same thing. Materialism, Jesus, whoever, they all say basically the same thing. "Material stuff is not important. The journey is important. Live now. Think now." They all think about happiness they just don't agree on the recipe of happiness, but they all say there is a recipe for happiness. Look at the best sellers, a lot of best sellers on the *New York Times* list. It's all the same thing. It's classical stuff that philosophers [said] 2,500 years ago and people read them. On the trail, you can experience it. I think you just taste it a bit and you just, you start, you finally appreciate the moment now. And this thing, the journey, yes, yes. I think a lot of people, suddenly their life changes because they started, for the first time they really understand. They can read the recipe or some of the recipes and then they suddenly start to discover a new perspective. It's incredible.

When Spirit first decided that she was going to attempt a thru-hike, she contacted Steven "Notes" Jones, a journalist in Atlanta, Georgia, who had thru-hiked in 2003. In his reply he wrote something similar to what Montreal described: hiking the Appalachian Trail "is a very spiritual experience. . . . You may not be religious but you are going to go through something on this trail."

From what both Graceful and Spirit suggest, as well as Montreal and others, spirituality is broadly defined on the Appalachian Trail. For example, whereas many who hike for spiritual reasons do so in the hopes of getting "closer to God," others find their spiritual connections within nature or the trail itself. Rez Dog considered "the natural world to be an expression of the Creator." He admitted that for him, being out in the woods on the trail was like being in church—the trail was his cathedral. Like many others mentioned previously, Rez Dog also noted the connection between hiking the Appalachian Trail and religious pilgrimage. He further suggested that the experience of hiking the trail has the power to "take you somewhere different, transcendental," for those willing to make the journey.

Trail Angels and Missionaries

Those familiar with the Appalachian Trail and hikers' spiritual motivations are aware that many come to the trail seeking answers or refuge or even God in the wilderness. They also recognize that many long-distance hikers are at a crossroads of sorts, or a transitional stage in life. As a result, individuals in the form of trail angels and missionaries, and religious organizations, position themselves to provide comfort and encouragement for hikers on their journey. For example, trail magic in the form of cold soft drinks and snacks was left on the trail in Tennessee, just after a road crossing, by young people, grades 1–6, from Nelson Chapel Baptist Church in 2013. A pink piece of paper was laminated and left on a tree above a cooler. The pink note read: "Help yourself to a drink and a snack. We pray for you hikers—for your health, safety, and that you grow closer to God during your time in His great outdoors."

Other trail angels, or rather, missionaries, may make themselves available should hikers want to talk about any spiritual or internal battles that may have brought them to the Appalachian Trail in the first place. Hatchet Jack shared a story about a couple of trail angels who invited him and two other hikers into their home for a three-course meal. In return, they just wanted to talk to them "a little bit about God." He found it amazing that someone would invite a "dirty, smelly hiker" into their home and offer him books to read, a bed, and home-cooked meal.

While many hikers have positive experiences with trail angels, like Hatchet Jack, this is not the case for everyone. Kutsa had a less-than-pleasant experience in town after receiving a ride from someone she initially thought was a trail angel:

> The first year I hiked, somewhere down, I won't say the name of the town because you [may] use that. I was hiking in Georgia and it snowed and I didn't have the right clothing. . . . I was like hypothermic. I got to this road totally frozen, and I had a ride from this guy. He's like totally excited. I told him I was

from Israel and he's like, "Wow, you're a real Jew from Israel." I said "yeah," and he's like running at 100 miles per hour down this windy road. I just wanted to get to a hotel. I was really sick, and he took me all over town, all over, he stopped everywhere and took me in different places saying, "Have you ever seen a real Jew, a real Jew from Israel?" [He says] they don't blame me for killing Jesus. And he gave cards. He was the chairman of the KKK in the next town. Yep. Then he told me he knew of a hotel and finally, after hours, I was half dead. Finally, I got to my hotel, and he knew what room I was in because he entered with me to talk to the lady at the entrance for an hour about my Jewish thing and no horns and all that, and he called me at 11:00 at night, I was shivering, to try to convince me to come to church the next day so he can show me [off to everyone]. At 12:00 he calls me again because he wanted me to talk to his wife. Then he came three days later, because I was really sick, three days later to take me up to the trail. He took me back and gave me his New Testament, prayed with me and all that, and for months I met hikers passing me [saying], "Oh, you're the girl from Israel, we heard about you from the Reverend."

Kutsa was not bitter about her experience with "the Reverend" in the least. She laughed the whole time she shared this story and talked about how much she loved her "community experiences." Encounters like this are probably few, but I think she may have had a run-in with a "trail devil," someone seeking to harm long-distance hikers or sabotage their hiking experience.

The number of trail angels, or in some cases missionaries, a hiker has the opportunity to interact with far outweighs the number of trail devils. As I mentioned earlier, trail angels and missionaries are aware that many hikers leave their former lives behind to seek refuge on the Appalachian Trail. Clay and Branch hike the Appalachian Trail together as part of a hiking ministry. They know that many people hike the trail searching for answers or searching for their purpose in life. As Clay, an ordained Baptist minister, stated:

A lot of people will get to Mount Katahdin, touch the sign, and think that they'll have more answers to life's questions. But, a lot of times they don't. So there're a number of hikers that hike the trail again and again wanting to find those answers. So we try to meet their physical needs first, like showers and medical needs. I'm an ordained minister and I've been trained in counseling, so we do counseling as well, and we meet their spiritual needs last.

As Clay explained it to me, he and Branch aim to live by example, and their initial goal is to provide a service to hikers. They follow the Golden Rule— "Do unto others as you would have them do unto you." If they are about to hike the two-tenths of a mile downhill for water, they will ask if anyone else needs water. They also told me that they do not approach hikers "to witness" to them or to talk about God but rather wait for hikers to bring these topics to them. Branch said that usually happens after they have been hiking with people for a while and get to know them. Eventually those who have questions open up and ask.

With their ministry, Clay and Branch often find themselves at Trail Days, where their church sets up a mobile unit to provide hikers with hot showers. I was one of the fortunate who experienced this generosity. Another religious congregation represented at Trail Days offers free medical services to hikers (see fig. 9). Specifically, they provide doctors and nurses who tend blisters, diagnose foot and knee problems, screen for skin

9. Two hikers receive medical treatment for blisters from professionals who volunteer their time during the 2007 Trail Days festival in Damascus, Virginia. Photograph by author.

cancer and dehydration, and provide BMI measurements, in addition to other services.

Hiking ministries such as these are continuing to grow, especially at Trail Days. At the festival in 2013, a church-affiliated mobile unit set up at the entrance to Tent City, where they offered soap, towels, and a hot shower. This same group also offered to wash and dry dirty hiking clothes for free. All we had to do was drop off our clothes, leave our trail name, and come back two to three hours later. Other religious organizations were offering free meals, free haircuts, and complimentary coffee, or free sewing of torn or damaged clothing.

Although most trail ministries tend to focus on meeting hikers' basic needs first, other individuals are more aggressive in meeting hikers' perceived spiritual needs. For example, this year at Trail Days, two other hikers and I were approached by two men and one woman who wanted to pray with us. They proceeded to ask us what was on our minds, making the assumption that we were lost or searching for something missing in our lives. The three continued on about how talking to God was like talking to our fathers and wondered what was heavy on our hearts that we might like to pray about or talk to the Father about that evening. It was at this point I told them that we were here to observe the hiking community as part of a sociology class, that we were not the "typical" hiker they may have been looking to speak with. They asked if they could pray with us anyway and wished us a safe weekend.

Trail Days and Tent City are not the only places where hikers may encounter individuals associated with a hiking ministry. Just as we approached a road crossing in southern Virginia, we were greeted by a Methodist minister, his wife, and four small children (the young pastor and his family from Star City, Arkansas, introduced in chap. 2), who work with a local Methodist church near Bastian, Virginia, each summer for two weeks as part of the Appalachian Trail Outreach Ministry (or ATOM). They were all wearing T-shirts bearing the atom symbol, with small hiker images used to represent electrons. I had the opportunity to chat with them as they grilled hotdogs and hamburgers for hikers passing through. They, too, were part of a hiking ministry because they knew that many come to the wilderness, to the Appalachian Trail, looking for answers or seeking God. The minister from Virginia also offered small Bibles to those who wanted one, commenting that he had done his research and found the lightest Bible possible. He knew how concerned hikers are with their pack weight.

Hikers may also interact with members of religious congregations when they stay in hostels, particularly when in towns to resupply, because the vast majority of these hostels are operated by religious organizations, including Methodist, Presbyterian, Episcopal, Baptist, and Catholic churches. There is also a Franciscan monastery in New York where hikers can stay, as well as a hiker hostel in Rutland, Vermont, operated by the Twelve Tribes Community. So, just as pilgrims may stay in hostels when on their spiritual journey, so too can long-distance hikers.

When I was staying with the Twelve Tribes, the person in charge of the hostel and who greeted hikers told us that he had once attempted a south-bound thru-hike but had never completed it. Ranon, the name given to him once he became a member of the Twelve Tribes Community, admitted to having some personal struggles and addictions that had led him to leave his job for the Appalachian Trail, as do many others. When he arrived in Rutland to resupply, he stayed at this hostel and never left. Ranon, with his new Hebrew name meaning "joyful," acknowledged he had found what he was looking for within the Community and no longer felt lost.

Sacred Texts

Unlike Ranon, who discovered himself and what he was looking for fairly early upon his removal from society, most hikers do not experience this revelation as quickly or as easily. Many long-distance hikers will carry sacred or religious texts to assist them as they navigate this new environment. Spirit saw "quite a few people with their Bibles," although she said they did not directly talk about religion or why they were carrying a Bible with them. She admitted that she carried her own and was reading her Bible along the way. Happy Feet also carried a Bible, but on a CD along with about five other books, half of which were written by evangelists and others on positive thinking. Kodak had recently picked up a copy of the *Tao Te Ching*, the philosophical and religious teachings of Taoism. She believed she was beginning to feel a stronger connection to nature and that these teachings would guide her along this new path of understanding.

When we consider what texts hikers may carry and deem sacred, religious texts such as those just mentioned may be what first come to mind. While long-distance hikers may carry such texts, they may also carry books of instruction of a different sort—in this case, guidebooks, to help them navigate the trail. The most common book of instruction, or sacred text as it becomes to long-distance hikers, is David "Awol" Miller's *The A.T. Guide: A Handbook for Hiking the Appalachian Trail*. This text, published annually, provides hikers with mail-drop guidelines, hiking etiquette, Leave No Trace principles, directions on getting to the trailheads of Springer Mountain and Mount Katahdin, as well as suggestions for obtaining permits to hike in the Great Smoky Mountains and Shenandoah National Parks. The text points out various places of interest and locations of campsites and water sources, provides a profile map so hikers can anticipate elevation gain and loss, gives detailed town and service information (such as the location of outfitters, fast food outlets, grocery stores, transportation, shuttle services, movie theaters, physicians, etc.), in addition to suggesting ways to offer trail magic.

The Appalachian Trail Data Book by Daniel Chazin, also published annually, is now in its thirty-fifth edition. This text, though helpful, does not provide as much detail as others for careful, complete planning; many find the information extremely helpful, however, especially when paired with other texts like Awol's or *The Appalachian Trail Guide*, published for each state. Similar to the guidebook by Awol, Chazin's data book provides guidelines for low-impact hiking, Leave No Trace principles, as well as locations of campsites, shelters, and water. In addition, the data book provides information on hiker safety and the protocol for reporting trail emergencies. Collectively, all of these "sacred" texts provide hikers with the formally recognized "dos and don'ts" associated with hiking the Appalachian Trail. They are valuable tools or books of instruction for hikers who carry them and are often referenced multiple times a day.

These books of instruction offer some logistical guidance, but there really is no way to prepare for all that this quest or spiritual journey on the Appalachian Trail entails. Consider Rez Dog's experience as he reflects on his first thru-hike:

Last time, I had very specific things that played through my mind almost every day . . . a very dominant thought early on was about Vietnam because I served in combat in a war that I opposed. And hiking has always had a connection to that because when you walk in the woods it's the same as being in the jungle. So every day that would come through. And I'd always thought about that when I hiked, but I never really pursued it because the hikes always ended or when I was at home and this thought came up I could always put it aside because of job, family, or whatever I was doing. But out here I couldn't do that. Out here there was nothing else to occupy that so it just kept playing on my mind. How? Why? What did this mean?

Like Rez Dog, as long-distance hikers break from their previous identities and the world they know, and leave society, work, and family behind, whether they are prepared or not, they enter the second stage of religious pilgrimage, the stage where transition takes place.

RITES OF TRANSITION

The second stage of religious pilgrimage is known as the liminal stage. To be liminal is to be in a space or moment where one is suddenly marginal, betwixt and between, neither here nor there. Social norms for behavior are not clear, or at least not known, and relationships are unfamiliar. To negotiate this new space, long-distance hikers engage in several transitional rites. For hikers on the Appalachian Trail, these rites lead to the emergence of new identities and new relationships, which are further reinforced through ritual gatherings as hikers embark on their personal journeys.

Ritual Renaming and Conversion

As mentioned in chapter 3, a rite of passage for long-distance hikers on the Appalachian Trail is the adoption of a trail name. This process of renaming is significant, according to Lady Mustard Seed, because trail names are about "breaking down barriers and becoming a community and a family. Yeah, transition. Transformation of the self." According to Taz, "shedding your old name" and taking on a new identity is simply part of the transformative process for many long-distance hikers setting foot on the Appalachian Trail for the first time. Similarly, Hobo Joe suggested trail names are symbolic of a hiker's journey, as "a lot of people change when they get off the trail, and they're a different person when they're on the trail." Calling someone by a trail name, to him, helps reinforce this new identity.

From a biblical perspective, the act of naming is believed to speak to the essence of one's character and nature. Recall that Ranon was given a Hebrew name once he became part of the Twelve Tribes Community, a name that reflected his "joyful" nature. Lady Mustard Seed makes the same connection with trail names. She suggests they are significant because they "speak to the essence of what it is people are after," or why they are hiking the Appalachian Trail. She admits to being self-directed on this aspect as she chose her name, Lady Mustard Seed, to reflect "the calling of the Spirit to be outside."

Clay specifically addressed the connection between trail names and "biblical themes," though he suggests there is "definitely no conscious thought of somebody taking on a new name on the trail and relating it to a biblical theme." Like Lady Mustard Seed, however, Clay and his wife intentionally selected names that were purposeful and symbolic in a spiritual or religious sense:

BRANCH: My name is Branch. It was definitely something we chose. We thought about possibly getting it from somebody else, but we really wanted to have a name with meaning. Something that would both give us something to talk about and something inwardly that would be sort of a reminder. So my name Branch comes from a verse in the Bible which is John 15:5 and it goes, Christ is talking and it says I'm the vine and you're the branches. He who comes to me will bear much fruit. Apart from me you can do nothing. And so I wanted to be a reminder to myself that apart from God I can do nothing. And when I have hard days I have to remember that.

CLAY: Yeah, it's really funny. There are names that are meaningless on the trail or have some kind of characteristic about a person. I mean like Backdraft, you know. And then there are names that are given, of course, because there's some aspect or quality about a person and another thru-hiker gave it to them. Like she said, we wrestled with this for a long time but we wanted significance with our name and purpose so I went with Clay, like Georgia clay, because we are from Georgia and that's also a Romans 9 verse, and it talks about God molding us and making us how He wants us.

Though Clay was not convinced others might do so, he, Branch, Lady Mustard Seed, Spirit, Graceful, and others clearly adopt trail names that remind of their purpose for being on the trail and their desire to be closer to God.

Whether chosen by a hiker or bestowed upon him or her by another, trail names have the potential to provide insight into someone's "essence" or character. Lady Mustard Seed found it particularly interesting that "people would pick [a trail name] for themselves as opposed to having other people pick one for you." Bonzo, who has thru-hiked the Appalachian Trail on two occasions, is the one who gave my hiking partner his trail name. Because we were from Mississippi and because he was dirty, my hiking partner originally chose the trail name Dirty South. After our stretch on the Roller Coaster, which may be recalled from chapter 2, my hiking partner's knees were not holding up well, and Bonzo took us in for the weekend. Once in the van and on our way to grab a cheeseburger and a beer, my hiking partner kept saying "I'm gunna make it, I'm gunna make it," to which Bonzo replied, "If you didn't have a trail name, I'd name you Gunna."

Interestingly, the biblical concept of naming is associated with authority in that it denotes the power of the namer. As someone who has thru-hiked the trail, Bonzo has attained the highest status recognized by members of the hiking community on the Appalachian Trail, that of a thru-hiker or 2,000-miler. With this status comes prestige and authority, in this case the power to name, or more accurately rename, Dirty South, a novice hiker. Though there are no written rules, formal or informal, for the giving and receiving of trail names constructed around hiker status, my hiking partner accepted his new name without hesitation and was known as Gunna from that day forward.

Branch specifically referenced instances of biblical renaming or the alteration of a name, such as when "Saul became Paul and Jacob became Israel." Though I do not focus on Saul in terms of renaming (his name change is not as connected to his conversion, as it is for hikers), I note that his conversion to Christianity began while traveling the road to Damascus. Ironically, the transformative experiences for long-distance hikers, religious or otherwise, could also be said to occur on the road to Damascus—Damascus, Virginia, that is. In fact, most of the hikers I spoke with were at or past Damascus, and significant change or transformation had already begun to take place. Hikers were already thinking about and anticipating how their lives would change once they left the trail to return home.

The book of Genesis tells of the renaming of Jacob to Israel—which Branch referred to—as well as the renaming of Abram to Abraham. Both men were renamed by God, a figure of power and authority. For both, the renaming is associated with a positive change. Additionally, the renaming occurred as each man was moving, traveling to and from noteworthy places (that is, Canaan, the Promised Land, Egypt). For example, Abram, called Father, traveled from the Promised Land to Egypt and then back to the Promised Land. During his travels he was renamed Abraham, now called Father of Many, to symbolize the covenant between he and God. Similarly Jacob, meaning supplanter or servant, traveled from Canaan to his uncle's in Haran and then back. Once he returned to Canaan, and on the night before he was to meet his brother, God renamed him Israel, meaning master, reflecting his struggles with man and the Divine, at which he prevailed.

Similar to the renaming of Jacob (Israel) and Abram (Abraham), the renaming of long-distance hikers on the Appalachian Trail is considered a positive experience, or conversion, in that many are at a crossroads in life or searching for answers. Just as the new identities that emerge for hikers can be characterized as embodied experiences because they involve the physical aspects of hiking the trail, such is the case for these two men of the Bible who made journeys of their own.

Thus, the biblical process of renaming involves two components—significant change, which can be positive or negative, and an association with a place. Both of these components can be applied to hikers' customary renaming and later transformation. Here, Phoenix Rising recounts the story of how she was given her trail name and the meaning behind it:

> It started off just because on day 1 doing the approach trail nobody caught my name. They only caught where I was from, so when I was very slowly meandering into camp that night everybody was asking "Where's Phoenix?" because they had seen me but had never known my name. So I got the name Phoenix. When I hiked the approach trail I decided, it was in the rain, and I decided that I was going back down the approach trail the next day and I wasn't going to continue on and I don't need to do this. I am miserable, why should I be miserable for the whole summer. So the next morning after everybody, everyone tried to calm me down that night and convince me to stay and sleep on it, don't make a decision right now, that kind of thing. The next morning I rose up like the phoenix does and I continued on. The Rising kind of stuck.

The phoenix, a mythical bird, is said to live anywhere from five hundred to a thousand years. At the end of its life, the bird and its nest are consumed by flames, and from the ashes a young phoenix emerges.

Hikers' experiences of rebirth on the Appalachian Trail are not merely figurative, nor do they disappear after the hike is over. Many hikers report feeling "born again" while hiking the trail as well afterward. Bonzo offered his personal story of transformation:

> I was a straight-up asshole when I stepped on the trail. You wouldn't be sitting here if I was like I was in 1996. I would wake up cussing. I was on county, state, and federal probation. About five weeks into this I was thinking I liked it. I could do this. I'd been doing it for a month and a half. And I prayed about that hike like I do with big stuff in my life. That's where I take it to. And when I ask His permission to do this, He's like "Go for it." It's spiritual. It is to this day.

Bonzo admits his expectations "were met a lifetime over" on the Appalachian Trail. I ran into him again at Tent City during Trail Days 2013, and he still tells this story of transformation. After introducing him to two of my students, he proceeded to tell them about how the Appalachian Trail and "the Man Up There" have changed him. Before the trail, Bonzo's reputation was one he is not proud of; now, however, his life is 100 percent different. He continues to describe his life as "beautiful." He no longer drinks "two or three cases of beer a day . . . and has a lot of friends, good friends in all areas of life."

As I mentioned earlier, many hikers may begin their journey on the Appalachian Trail while dealing with some sort of struggle, personal or spiritual, and during the hike become a different person. But why does their departure from society for the Appalachian Trail result in such significant change? Why this road to Damascus? Gypsy Lulu offered one perspective:

> This is not true all across the board, but for me, I brought my conversations with God . . . with me. It didn't start on the trail, but for a lot of people it does. All of a sudden they're out here and they realize that "Wow, this God or higher being," whatever they would choose to call it, "I can't escape it out here." Nature, and I'm not saying that nature is the God, but nature speaks so loudly of God. And I'm not trying to proselytize you or anything, you're asking for it number one. And so here you are spending all day hiking in this season that is changing so rapidly and breathing life back into itself again, it almost screams of God. It's really amazing . . . for me, at least, I just want to explode. It just fills you in this very good way. And for me, I explode in praise.

For other people, I don't know how they deal with it. They might say, "Gee, this is incredible." For me, I take pictures, write about it, pull out my penny-whistle and play a little bit.

For Gypsy Lulu, nature and the environment speak "so loudly of God." Though she brought her habitual conversations with God onto the trail with her, she acknowledges that other hikers begin those conversations while on their journey, during their pilgrimage. Maybe the trail experience becomes sacred because as their natural environment changes, whether it is the seasons, the scenery, or varied weather patterns, they are changing too. Everything, including hikers, is in a constant state of flux.

Lady Mustard Seed offers another perspective as to why the Appalachian Trail is an environment conducive to change. She suggests that "the trail is an entity unto itself where the veil between us and God is much, much thinner." While hiking, she believed that God was bringing people into her life and that all of those she met, good and bad, were purposely brought to her to teach her something about herself.

Communitas Relationships

Most people who come to hike long distance on the Appalachian Trail begin their journey alone. There are a handful of couples or friends who may start together, but for the most part this is an individual journey in which hikers find themselves initially alone, away from home and family, away from relationships that made them feel secure. New relationships must now be established with complete strangers, and these relationships, as Señor Nobs says, become a significant part of the trail experience. When he reflects on his thru-hike, Señor Nobs admits it is always the people he remembers— not the terrain, not the views, but the people.

According to Phoenix Rising, relationships that develop among hikers during this stage of their journey are something "that you just don't see in the normal world, the normal American society." The fact that a complete stranger is willing to do whatever it takes to make another hiker's life easier is, to her, "an awesome, awesome thing." These sorts of relationships that emerge among hikers on the Appalachian Trail are best characterized by the word *communitas*. Relationships that are communitas are personal and immediate, emotional, natural and authentic, and collective and cooperative rather than individual and competitive (Turner 1974). From the descriptions proffered by many long-distance hikers, these are the bonds that unite members of the hiking community on the Appalachian Trail.

While many long-distance hikers enjoy their outdoor experience and the panoramic views, when asked what they most enjoyed about hiking the Appalachian Trail the overwhelming majority said the people or friends they met along the way. One hiker, Boone, initially "thought [other hikers] would be in the way," partly because "you are only going to know them for a day," which to him was somewhat "weird." Others like Turbo, however, were looking forward to meeting and hanging out with new people, although he admitted that it kind of wore on him after a while: "I like to hang out with people and spend time with people. That's one thing that's been kind of tough actually. Even if you spend three or four days with somebody, you know, one of you is planning on staying in a certain hostel or meeting somebody and then you may never see that person again. That's kind of strange and kind of hard to get used to." According to Turbo, relationships that develop among long-distance hikers can develop instantly, but they may also end as quickly as they started for a variety of reasons. Because of the changing nature of hikers' relationships, Skywalker refers to them as "loose associations":

> I read that most relationships form out here on the trail and that's definitely been true. I mean things happen fast and I reckon probably a lot of them break up fast to be quite honest, once you get off the trail. But what I have also noticed is you form these quick relationships and they tend to be very close, but people, especially thru-hikers, are very task-oriented, and if there's any significant difference at all, like in speed or schedules and so forth, people just move apart. They come back together when they do. You see a lot of people you recognize—you see loose associations that temporarily become close associations and then become loose associations again.

Graceful is one hiker who quickly formed strong attachments to people she met on the trail, a group of four sisters to be exact. She reflected on how she felt when they left after finishing their section hike in Damascus:

> I had gotten to be close to these sisters—there were four sisters out here, the Barefoot Bunch—and a day out here is equivalent to a week in the "real" world it feels like to me. I was hiking with them specifically for about a week,

and when they left it was like this sudden feeling of loss. My brother only knew them for two days, and he was feeling the same thing. They're great girls. They're hard core.

What Graceful experienced with the Barefoot Bunch was emotional, as well as personal and immediate. And this attachment happened after knowing them for only one week, which felt like much longer to her. Unfortunately, the relationship she established with the sisters ended just as quickly as it began. Phoenix Rising said that in her experience, and from what her friends have told her, you never really contact people you meet after you leave the trail. These friendships "really do stick to the trail," which she finds kind of sad.

Though Phoenix Rising's and her friends' experiences, as well as what Graceful and her brother experienced with the Barefoot Bunch, may be true for most, some relationships do last well beyond the Appalachian Trail. For those hikers "you make really good friends with, you end up finding out their real names and addresses and phone numbers," according to Little Cubit, a twenty-six-year-old hiker from South Carolina. Drifter also made lifelong friends when he was hiking the trail, like Otter, whom he considers his brother to this day. Kutsa and Montreal met on the Appalachian Trail at the true halfway point in Pennsylvania and later married. Their best man, Mr. Pink, is someone they met and became good friends with on the trail. Kutsa said the relationships she and others have developed and maintained are really sincere. Montreal offered a reason why:

Because you shared some fears . . . and you share some experience. Like I told you, you want to share this experience with people. A lot of times you go back home and unless they did something, unless they did the same thing, they don't really understand. And it's like the army. A guy going into Iraq or Vietnam can come back and tell people the stories and they listen, but they cannot really understand unless they've been there with him. This is why they have this connection between army people. "Oh, you did Vietnam, oh yeah, where were you?" They know. It's the same thing with hikers. You don't have to say it. We've been through a lot of this stuff before so we see people, "Oh, man, where were you? Oh, you did that?!?" You don't have to say it. You know what the guy is feeling. You know it. So, when you meet with these other people after there's this very tight bond. We keep in touch.

According to Kutsa, they were in a group of about eight hikers from all over who became close friends. Their relationships were authentic. They lived and worked together and became like family for a while. Graceful, though she did not keep in touch with the Barefoot Bunch, echoed Montreal and Kutsa's sentiment of being with family due to shared experiences: "Essentially, it's like a family in the fact that you might not have everything in common with your siblings or extended family, but you care about people and you love people for who they are and y'all are all part of something." Even the hikers Taz has yet to meet she considers "brothers and sisters in a way." Gus offered an interesting explanation, that the community was more of a "moving family. Everybody gets up in the morning and moves . . . but you all feel related." One reason may be that many of the supports family members provide one another—meeting another's emotional, social, and nutritional needs—are provided by fellow hikers—strangers according to Vogue—in the absence of family.

The hiking community cheers one another on and rallies behind one another to such an extent that some even leave the trail together when one is injured. Slick described such a situation: "There was a guy that I was just hearing about the other night over at the drum circle [at Tent City] who had to get off the trail with some really serious medical problems. I don't remember what started it or alerted him to it but he had to go into Johnson City over by Erwin and have a spinal tap and all this stuff. A handful of hikers got off and refused to go on just waiting with him. I mean this is someone they hadn't even known for that long." Here they are, hiking with people they do not really know, not even by birth names, yet these hikers leave the trail to support their new friend in a time of need. Slick continued, saying that this support system exists because hikers are "all going through the same thing out here, and you're with each other all the time," so the community becomes like an instant family.

Taz further noted: "We're leaning on each other, and when one's down we pull them up, and when we're down, they pull us back up. I'd say you need them." This is true. Because long-distance hikers are away from family, friends, and significant others for weeks or months at a time, many become homesick or lonely. For example, Little Cubit thought she would hike with others her age but found herself with middle-aged and older hikers, mostly men. She said most of them seemed lonely and wanted to share their life experience with someone, so they would open up and tell her about their daughters. It was almost as if they "became dad again," offering Little Cubit all of the advice they could possibly share.

Hikers not only support one another socially and emotionally. Happy Feet carried in fried chicken strips that he received from a trail angel to fellow hikers at a shelter. A few years ago, I passed Lion King, a former thru-hiker who had documented his hike in a video titled *Walking with Freedom*, as he was hiking southbound to Trail Days. He had purchased a few burgers from Burger King and was taking them to the shelter for hikers that night. Lady Mustard Seed specifically commented on the nutritional support hikers can provide to one another in times of need: "When you're out in the woods and everybody's hungry, everyone's low on food, and you're one day from town, and someone knows you're low on food says, 'Have one of my cookies'; that's trail magic (smiles). [Food is] a huge ration at that point, and stuff like that happens."

Though trail magic is typically given by trail angels in the form of a ride to town or large hiker feeds, fellow hikers can and do give trail magic to one another by sharing their food. Yet when hikers do give one another trail magic, they do not necessarily think of it in that way. For the most part, they simply offer a kind word of encouragement, share food, or carry an item they found in the hopes of finding its owner, which a member of the Barefoot Bunch did for me when I managed to lose a sandal that had been strapped to the back of my pack. One of the sisters found it and carried it a few miles, asking every hiker she passed if it belonged to him or her. Hikers perform these random acts of kindness for one another because a fellow hiker would do it for them.

So, even though these makeshift families have the potential to change daily, hikers develop strong attachments to and cooperative relationships with one another and the hiking community on the Appalachian Trail. These new relationships, and subsequently identities, are further strengthened when hikers have opportunities to come together.

Ritual Gatherings

When fellow hikers come together at "sacred" sites, they dance, tell stories of adventure, of hiker traditions, of trail magic, or talk about the many heroes and legends that have come to be associated with the Appalachian Trail. These collective experiences or opportunities, planned or spontaneous, further reinforce the new identities and relationships that emerge for long-distance hikers during the transitional stage. Lady Mustard Seed described how it felt for her coming into Damascus for Trail Days, the largest planned gathering of long-distance hikers:

Coming into Damascus has been a lot of fun because you see people that we saw in the beginning, and it's so great that they're still on. It's a strong community, like we were saying earlier. It's amazing because you're forming bonds, and it's not based around alcohol or anything altering your perceptions—but your perceptions are kind of altered because you're in the woods, and your senses are kind of deprived, and you're working so hard for a common goal. That's what all your friendships are rallying behind, and you get a sense of who's ahead of you and who's behind you, and you're all rooting for each other. So, it certainly lifts my spirits to run into someone that we haven't seen in several days. And it was a lot of fun throwing water balloons at each other today. It's great to come into town and walk into a bar and see someone you haven't seen in three days. So, thru-hikers have definitely lifted our spirits. . . . It's a very strong sense of community that I probably haven't experienced since high school sports . . . something similar . . . a feeling.

As an annual event, this ritual gathering of hikers clearly reinforces a feeling of camaraderie and community as Lady Mustard Seed suggested, which is essential for every society, every subculture. To borrow from sociologist Emile Durkheim, this feeling can best be described as "collective effervescence" or an extremely intense emotional connection that emerges when groups come together. In the case of long-distance hikers, a kind of electricity is generated that reinforces the social bonds among members of the hiking community. This feeling cannot be achieved by one person alone, and it fades as hikers leave Trail Days to continue their individual journeys; it returns, however, at the next opportunity hikers have to come together. Looking over my personal journal from 2005, I came across the following passage about my own experience at Trail Days that same year:

This community thing hikers speak of . . . I'm a little jealous. Starting to feel like a part of it now but a little far away or detached from the whole experience. But it's nice hearing hikers tell their stories . . . again I'm jealous. I wish I could have been with them. BUT besides that, I know I'll make my own experiences soon enough. What I find I am getting from the hikers is mostly inspiration.

I'm so inspired by them. I find myself beginning—not so much beginning I guess—but on the verge of starting my own personal journey or discovery.

I was an outsider at the time I wrote this paragraph; I did not yet feel a part of the hiking community. I certainly would not have been thought of as a thru-hiker, since I had not started with the pack at Springer and had not established relationships with other hikers. I merely existed among them. I had a trail name, one I was given in 1999, but that was not enough to solidify my belonging as I was only beginning my hike that summer. For that matter, I had not even begun to experience any transformation; nor did I expect that would happen. I continued writing: "I loved hearing and seeing the hikers get together around here, playing music and singing, some dancing. I know a lot more went on at Tent City—maybe next time I can take in that experience." The hikers I am writing about were sitting outside of The Place, the hostel in Damascus operated by the local Methodist church, where hikers spontaneously come together during Trail Days. Since then, I have had the opportunity to experience Tent City, a geographical oddity in itself.

At Tent City, hikers are allowed to set up tents near the baseball field; there is also a tent village located in the woods surrounding the perimeter of the ball field. In this village, hikers from previous years, who come about a week early, set up their "cities." Some examples are Billville, Pound Town, and Riff Raff, each "city" with its own vibe. For example, beer pong and poker were common at this year's Pound Town. The Jolly Roger flag, with the familiar skull and crossbones, identified the city Riff Raff. Here hikers commonly shout "riff raff" before entering or risk being turned away by the "mayor," a former hiker donning a sport coat and tie.

The several drum circles and campfires held each night within the woods at Tent City are strikingly similar to a corroboree, "a noisy festivity" with song and dance held by Australian aborigines to celebrate important events. I can certainly attest to the fact that the "natives" seemed restless: the drums and shouting continued until the wee hours of the morning, as Trail Days was quickly coming to a close. Life, or more accurately backpacking for most, would resume as normal the next day.

While festivals like Trail Days are among the planned gatherings that allow the hiking community to come together, there are plenty of random gatherings that are just as meaningful. Sunshine reflected that some of her highest points on the trail included not only the day she hiked her personal record of seventeen miles, but also a spontaneous meeting of hikers that took place at Pine Grove Furnace State Park: "Just everyone that we've been reading, your entries and Gus's entries and HeartFire's entries and T-Mac and Turbo, we all just came together in this one place and had an awesome afternoon with ice cream. Everyone was just hanging out and having a good time. Just the fact that everyone we were reading about came together." We all "came together" at the Pine Grove Furnace Store, near the official halfway point of the Appalachian Trail, for the traditional Half Gallon Challenge.

Random gatherings like those just described provide additional opportunities for hikers to share their trail adventures. So does meeting up at night around the shelters that dot the entirety of the trail. At each shelter, and in most hostels, there is a shelter journal, a notebook and pen usually found in a plastic bag. Upon arrival, hikers will locate the journal, sign in, and read other hikers' entries. Sunshine hinted at this ritual of sorts, which reinforces hikers' new relationships and identities. These journals could also be considered "sacred texts," a form of "trail scripture," which hikers read daily. Some might even say these entries are a source of inspiration for current and future hikers.

In the trail journals, hikers discuss a variety of topics. Many have ongoing debates about religion, discuss conspiracy theories, leave confessions, write poetry, tell jokes and leave the punch line in the journal to follow, or let hikers know about the terrain or any "unfriendlies" in the area. The following is an entry written by Amos Anon on April 1, 2005, at Niday Shelter in response to the statement, "Tell me a conspiracy theory":

> I set out to the woods last night to bury some demons. Not the physical, but those that are twice as real, only in my head. Fear is a paralyzing yet necessary emotion. For nearly a decade fear has plagued my psyche. Attempts to bury fear, be it with distractions or substances, are only futile although admittedly fun. Fortunately inspired by the wisdom of a thru-hiker I found the courage to find myself. I admit putting your heart on the line and giving nothing but your all is terrifying, but it's the only way to live. Make your life a walking work of art!
>
> Perhaps I am an alcoholic, but hey "If you can't join 'em, beat 'em." You can become an adult and still remain young, you just can't stay childish.
>
> Oh, yeah, a conspiracy theory: I believe George Bush and Osama bin Laden suffer from the same complex. Trust in God is a great thing, but

believing you must manifest His greatness with absolute certainty will only result in the loss of God and the entrance of man's corruption.

May this trail allow you to find your own path.

Like many, Amos Anon is hiking the Appalachian Trail to "bury some demons" while also searching for answers. He identified in some way with a former thru-hiker and was inspired to leave everything behind to hike the trail. Like others, he also seems to be battling addiction, if we are to believe the sincerity of his entry. Hikers who read this passage in the journal may find a connection with Amos, in terms of his inner struggles and reasons for hiking the trail. Others who do not still may find humor, perhaps confirmation, in his discussion of conspiracy theories, or even inspiration to follow their own dreams.

Hikers may also use shelter journals to share lessons they have learned or offer suggestions for "good behavior," as Sweet Sixteen did in the journal at Trimpi Shelter on May 19, 2005:

The kindest thing a hiker can do on the trail is to share his water with someone in need—thanks Underground, Fester, and Pete.

P.S. Shower and pizza tonight! Is this heaven?

For many long-distance hikers, the Appalachian Trail is indeed a little slice of heaven. Sweet Sixteen's heaven may be the pizza, the shower, or even the camaraderie, if not all three. Some hikers use the shelter journal to confide in others, which at times is easier to do with strangers. The Priest Shelter is one such "sacred" place, where hikers leave written confessions in the journal there. Some confessions may be humorous, whereas others may be personal testimonies or discussions of "sins" recently committed by the writers and detailed in hopes of forgiveness by "The Priest."

Daily opportunities to sit back and "break bread" with fellow hikers, like sharing mealtime together nightly at shelters, or even ice cream, also strengthen bonds among members of this community. Numerous hikers have told me how being on the trail and interacting with hikers, as well as trail angels, has restored their faith in the goodness of humankind. I would have to agree. The kindness of strangers, and how quickly relationships develop on the Appalachian Trail, is truly amazing. Returning home from an environment in which people feel accepted for who they are and where learning to trust blindly in the kindness of strangers is part of the journey can make for an interesting experience when the hike is over.

Montreal likens hikers' retreat into the woods and reincorporation into society as an initiation rite of sorts:

> For a lot of people the trail is almost like an initiation rite the way you are by yourself in the forest for days and then you [are] reaccepted by the community. I think a lot of people don't have faith in the modern world or the rites we have—weddings, communion, stuff like that—they're not as powerful as they were, so I think a lot of people rediscover that on the trail, you know, to be able to be by yourself and rediscover your body and how you survive.

As long-distance hikers are "reaccepted" into society, they bring with them new identities that now must unite, or possibly compete, with old ones left behind. Yet we must not forget that long-distance hiking is also an embodied experience. Hikers must also adjust physically, not just mentally and socially, to life after the Appalachian Trail.

RITES OF INCORPORATION

In the third or postliminal stage of the journey, long-distance hikers are reintroduced back into society, the world they left behind. "Reentry" as Drifter referred to it, can be difficult as hikers are faced with managing multiple identities, new and old, simultaneously. At the same time, this can be a positive experience. Hobo Joe recognized that "from here, there are a million different ways you can go" and that many people continue on to lead different lives after they have hiked the Appalachian Trail as a result of discovering "what they really love to do." This discovery, he believes, is an important part of the journey too.

Newfound Simplicity

As long-distance hikers remove themselves from the working world and the multiple roles or identities they occupy in society and spend time on the trail, they have a chance to sort through their lives. For some long-distance hikers, their experience on the Appalachian Trail finds them looking for a new career upon return. Phoenix Rising seemed to have had an epiphany while on the trail. Laughing, she said:

> I learned I cannot go back to corporate America. That's definitely not for me. I really learned that I definitely need to change my career path, and I think I'm actually going to go back to school for massage therapy, sports trainer, physical therapist, something along those lines because I need to be doing something that I'm helping others with. I just can't have one of those classically corporate jobs and be happy. Being out here, especially now that I'm getting lower on funds and trying to make it stretch as long as possible because I want to stay out here and help people that much more, makes me really realize I need to be doing something along those same lines when I'm back in the real world.

Phoenix Rising had a Bachelor of Science in aircraft crash investigation and was working for an insurance company in Arizona insuring aircraft. After her time on the Appalachian Trail, she realized that she needed or wanted a change, one that would allow her to help people in some way. Corporate America did not fulfill that need for her. Montreal suggested that this was because after hiking the trail, "a lot of people come back to their work, and a lot of things seem ridiculous. You hear your boss freak out about stuff, and it's so ridiculous. It's numbers on paper, and in the woods, you have to boil your water."

Laughing, Montreal said that hiking the Appalachian Trail often leads to a change in one's outlook on life, as it did for Phoenix Rising. When he was working on a film set upon his return home, people were screaming, "Where's the actor? Where's the actor? We're ready on set. Where's the actor?" While all of this was going on, Montreal was in the process of taking off his walkie-talkie and thought to himself, "Children are dying in the world right now, and this isn't really important, all this crap." What was once considered important, such as "numbers on paper" or the location of actors for a shoot, now seemed ridiculous to Montreal, especially if that was all people really cared about in the world. According to Obie, a return thru-hiker in his midforties, simplifying one's life allows hikers to step back and realize what is really significant and important to them, not necessarily what is important to others, which can often be the case at work.

Phoenix Rising continued to wonder about how her life might have been different, what paths she might have taken, had she hiked the Appalachian Trail in her twenties or even teens:

> I know people who have done it younger and now are living a much different lifestyle than the average American lives and part of me is jealous of that because I think if I had started earlier, where would I be today? How much happier would I have been for the last ten years than just kind of subsiding as an average American? But, I think, I definitely see just big changes. I'm trying to avoid going back to the real world because I've had so much fun out here that I just don't want to do it, you know. I see big changes, though, for me in the future.

Phoenix Rising, like Montreal, suggests that many people rediscover things about themselves because they are "outside of their social environment," the one they have grown accustomed to in the "real world." Lady Mustard Seed attempts to describe the "real world" lifestyle and why the Appalachian Trail makes rediscovery possible:

> Your whole life in town is focused on sustaining your life in town. We work forty plus hours a week to sustain a certain lifestyle, and that lifestyle is exhausting. It's hard to work forty hours. After I work my job I'm exhausted on the weekend. I don't have the energy to give back to my family, to myself, to God. And retreating into the woods, just leaving all of these obligations, leaving everything behind specifically just to seek and just to be with nature is a complete shift in focus.

For the two missionaries, Clay and Branch, the transition from trail life to the "real world" was miserable and unsettling. On their first trip to the Appalachian Trail, Branch admits they were not prepared for the transition to home because their hike was cut short by three months. They had no idea where they would go or what they were going to do next. Even a trip to the grocery store was nerve-racking and nearly "caused a heart attack because people [were] running" by them.

As a result of their experience, what might even be considered culture shock, Clay and Branch make sure that anyone they send to the trail as part of their hiking ministry is prepared for the "transitional state that you'll go through in order to assimilate into society, regular society." Thinking about this transition, Gus found himself getting a little nervous at the thought of going home: "Actually it's been kind of difficult because, even like with staying here in this hostel, I find it almost confining. To get back into your routine, to get back into a confining little house, you fear that you may never get back to what we have on the trail. It makes you nervous."

Though Little Cubit had heard that some people, like Clay and Gus, "feel claustrophobic or out of place" when leaving the trail, she had not experienced those feelings as yet. Of course, she acknowledged, she might feel that way when she left the trail to spend a few days in New York City. The pace of life for Clay, Branch, and Gus had slowed on the trail. They were no longer accustomed to the rat race associated with modern society. Graceful, too, found herself becoming frustrated with cars and traffic the more time she spent on the trail. Even Drifter talked about how hard it was for him to adjust to a more structured environment—"to punching clocks, to having people tell you what to do, how to do."

Regardless of whether "reentry" is positive or negative, or is related to work or a change in one's outlook on life, most hikers experience some sort of change in lifestyle upon returning home. For some hikers, the change involves a different career path or business venture; for others, it means more long-distance hiking.

Physical Transformations

Given the strenuous nature of long-distance hiking, hikers are bound to experience some physical changes upon their return to society. As hikers go through the process of reentry, their bodies need time to adjust. Excessive food consumption, for example, is common among long-distance hikers, and this habit can be difficult to break when the hike is over. Hikers have grown accustomed to ingesting thousands of calories per day, much of it in the form of protein and carbohydrates.

Hiking into Erwin, Tennessee, this year, I passed a hiker who had thru-hiked the Appalachian Trail two years prior. I asked why he was hiking again, and he told me it was to lose weight. He had lost fifty pounds his first time out, but he gained over seventy pounds upon return. I commented jokingly, "So, you still ate as if you were hiking the trail, huh?" to which he smiled and replied, "Oh, yeah." For Clay, he said it was "interesting to see

TV again and all the 'lose weight now' type of stuff. We're like, just go hike the trail, it's all you can eat and lose all your weight."

During her first long-distance hike, Kutsa lost one hundred pounds, was healthy, and said she was in the best shape of her life. When she returned home, one thing she missed about being on the Appalachian Trail was "being free and being hungry." Kutsa talked about how she'd been over-weight her entire life, often feeling sedated by food. She has been battling her weight and has been on diets since she was five years old, something she says most people could not even begin to understand.

Hiking the Appalachian Trail would appear to be a win-win situation for those wanting to lose weight. Weight loss on the trail is something that occurs without the least bit of effort. Once hikers return home, however, they must change and monitor their eating habits if they wish to maintain their weight loss, an unexpected benefit of hiking for some, but perhaps a bit of work for others.

Another habit some long-distance hikers develop on the trail would be considered unhealthy, and it is a difficult habit to break upon return-ing home. Contrary to what might be expected given the strenuous nature of long-distance hiking, Gypsy Lulu said that some people actually begin smoking cigarettes on the trail:

> I don't smoke . . . but I hang out with a lot of people that smoke. I've talked to a lot of past thru-hikers that started smoking just because of the bugs that were so bad and they don't bother you if you're smoking . . . and you go, "What was the biggest shock as far as a change in your behavior? Well, I became a nicotine addict because of mosquitoes." Well that was unexpected. You don't hear that from the Go Lite table.

As Gypsy Lulu noted, hikers do not learn about smoking to keep the bugs at bay from vendors, such as Go Lite or Osprey, at Trail Days. A campfire would do the trick, but gathering wood and building one takes more work, especially for someone who has hiked over twenty miles. I have also heard that for those who do smoke, they learn to roll their own cigarettes, and those who already roll their cigarettes learn to do it one-handed. Of course, other hikers, like my hiking partner Gunna, kick the habit altogether. Whether one is a smoker or nonsmoker, this behavior change will often require some adjustment upon return.

Because hiking the Appalachian Trail can be a transformative experience in any number of ways, some hikers may mark their bodies with a tattoo once their hike is over. It is not uncommon for long-distance hikers to tattoo the Appalachian Trail symbol, their trail name, or something symbolic of their experience on their bodies. This act gives them an outward symbol or reminder of their journey or spiritual quest. For example, Bramble, a return thru-hiker and self-proclaimed "homeless nomad" from Connecticut in his early thirties, tattooed the AT symbol on the third finger of his left hand after his initial thru-hike. When asked why, he replied: "Because I have always wanted to be married for fifty years to the day I die. I figured out here Mother Nature's my mother and God is my father. And I can always be married to Mother Nature, she'll always be here. Out here I feel more at peace." The AT symbol serves as a reminder of Bramble's experiences on the trail, a place where he feels at peace, even safe. He had recently divorced prior to his thru-hike, which also might have influenced his choice in tattoo and its placement.

While Bramble had the AT symbol tattooed on his body, at least one hiker I know of had the entire trail tattooed on his:

It came to me in a dream. Didn't I tell you about that? I had a dream Angus Young was hiking out in front of me. The lead guitarist for AC/DC. And he's got his backpack on, and I can see the front of his guitar, you know, the back of it. You know how he plays, right? And I'm hiking behind him in full-length blue jeans, which, you know, you don't hike the trail in full-length blue jeans, had sandals on, no shirt, but the trail was on my back. And I woke up and I'm in that exact moment.

Two weeks before Trail Days in 1998, Bonzo had the Appalachian Trail tattooed on his back as a result of this dream. This was one year after his first thru-hike. He told me he is now able to carry his trail experience with him forever on his back. When he dies, he also knows where he wants to be buried on the trail—near a set of rocks at Apple Orchard Shelter, an old hay barn.

Like Bramble and Bonzo, I decided to get a tattoo upon return, one that would serve as a reminder of my trail experience. I wanted something that would remind me that when things get tough, life is not so bad after all and there is a lot of good in the world. I needed and wanted that constant reminder, especially on occasions when I found myself around negative people, people who complained too much, or who always seemed to find fault in others. Basically, the complete opposite of what I had come to expect of people I met and interacted with hiking the Appalachian Trail.

A New Me

In addition to career changes and bodily transformations, long-distance hikers also make social adjustments as they return to mainstream society. In other words, when hikers leave the Appalachian Trail, whether it is after a thru-hike or a section hike, relationships with others, even those considered "good" friends, may change. As Montreal noted, "People welcome you back home . . . but they cannot share the experience you've been through. You would like to talk about it, but they cannot grasp it." Montreal continued to describe this new lack of connection he experienced with people he had been "very good friends with for a long time":

> People that you know, their life was their job, and they come on the trail and they go back and suddenly things that were important are not necessarily important. You go back and talk to your friends and your friend suddenly talks about stuff that has interested you for twenty years and then you listen to them and you're thinking, "You're so boring. I'm sorry but that's not my life anymore."

Some of these relationships, like those Montreal refers to, may even dissolve because people change or find they have less in common after their hike. Montreal suggests that this lack of connection or understanding with friends back home is why people return to Trail Days year after year, become trail angels, return to hike sections of the trail, or begin to do trail maintenance. They want to "redo the experience, and [because] they cannot share [their trail experiences] with their [home] community," they go back to the Appalachian Trail with the people who understand. This is one reason why some return to give trail magic to the current year's class of hikers. As Drifter explained: "There's a lot more people who have done the AT. They've experienced trail magic, and it was so good for them at the time that they want to give back a little bit. I've done my share over the years and a big part of the reason for wanting to do trail magic is because you know how much it is appreciated by the hikers."

While some past thru-hikers, like Drifter, may come back to give trail magic, others come back to hike time and again. Graceful met a guy named Seiko, "Seiko like the watch," who reportedly has been hiking the Appalachian Trail for sixteen years. Seiko hikes a little, goes back to work for a few months, and returns again. Depending on whom you ask, Seiko has hiked anywhere from 15,000 to 30,000 miles on the trail, leading some to doubt the authenticity of his claim. Warren Doyle, however, is a well-known hero and legend of the Appalachian Trail, having hiked over 34,000 miles, the equivalent of hiking the trail sixteen times. He claims to have hiked the AT more than anyone else. Graceful herself admits there are days where she thinks that if she reached Katahdin, she would turn around and do the hike all over again and understands why people do.

Montreal further asserted that people come back to hike long-distance because in society people tend to "earn their rites traditionally," whereas hikers on the Appalachian Trail go through a different sort of "initiation." Montreal suggested that once northbound hikers, or NOBOs, summit Katahdin, they leave with the impression that "they conquered the universe," that they will reenter society and be thought of as heroes. As he explained it, once they return home after completing a thru- or section hike on the Appalachian Trail, many hikers are still there on the trail, at least to the extent their minds will allow.

Personally it takes me a couple of weeks to adjust to life back home after spending a few weeks on the trail, particularly when interacting with strangers. When hiking the trail, you get so used to people, trail angels, offering you rides to town. Once I was leaving a friend's house and two young college-aged men offered me a ride home. It was about 10:30 at night, and I was only about a half mile from my apartment. Without hesitation, I thanked them and hopped into the backseat. When the doors automatically locked, I thought, "What was I thinking? I am no longer on the trail!" I quickly realized, though this experience did not turn out badly, that trail life is not the same as "real life," as Lady Mustard Seed said. I brought that sense of trust home with me, of trusting in the kindness of strangers.

I have been told by others to "take my rose-colored glasses off," but seeing the goodness in people and trusting them is simply who I am today. When traveling to West Virginia for a job interview at Marshall University, my flight was delayed, which meant my ride from Charleston to Huntington had to be rearranged. I was advised to take a cab and would be reimbursed later. Just as I was departing the plane in Charleston, I asked a couple next to me roughly what the gratuity would be for a cab ride that distance, to which they replied, "You're only going to Huntington? You can ride with us. We live just over the river in Ohio and are going that way." My quick response was "Thank you." I never hesitated. When I told my husband about this, he said, "Please do not tell anyone at Marshall you took a ride from total strangers." Clearly, the trail experience, if the transformation was meaningful, can become a part of one's identity and can influence interactions with others long after the hike is over.

EPIPHANIES IN ITHAKA

This pilgrimage or journey for long-distance hikers is similar to the one taken by the Greek hero Odysseus after the Trojan War. Odysseus, king of Ithaka, wandered the world for ten years before returning to his homeland. During his travels, Odysseus had many adventures, endured several challenges, and learned life lessons that would change him greatly. The poem "Ithaka," written in 1911 by Greek poet C. P. Cavafy, captures this voyage of self-discovery (Jusdanis 1987). Whether section hiking or thruhiking the Appalachian Trail, long-distance hikers find themselves on a journey similar to Odysseus's, one that is often transformative in nature, from spiritual to physical, emotional to social, or some combination. One might even wonder if these changes are sincere and enduring or if the honeymoon is over quickly upon return? I have no doubt the change is temporary for some and real and lasting for others. Take Bonzo, for instance. He is now proud of the reputation he has today, which is something he could not have said in the past. A younger Drifter, however, told me that although he changed somewhat the previous year during his hike, it was "hard not to get back into the same old routines and habits" once he returned home.

I imagine most hikers expect and assume their transformation will be noticeable and take place quickly as they move through each stage of their pilgrimage. Montreal, however, argued that what people learn about themselves and about the world as a result of their hike of the Appalachian Trail comes to them gradually over time rather than instantaneously:

I think it's not when you arrive at Katahdin [that] you really gain something from the trail. I think it's during the first three months or six months or a year after. You have to absorb it. It's like water with mud. Things have to settle, and then when you rethink about it six months, a year, three years later; then there's a feeling. It's very abstract. I don't think you gain something when you're at the end. I think you gain something after thinking about the journey or feeling the journey that you've been through. It's very abstract but I think it's very real because I've talked to a lot of people about it. A lot of them felt proud on top of Katahdin, the picture and all, but you didn't gain something. You gain it after.

For many pilgrims on this northbound journey, the final, climatic goal is reaching Mount Katahdin. For some, the journey ends there, depending on their reasons for hiking. What Montreal seems to be suggesting, though, is that the postliminal stage of pilgrimage does not have an endpoint. Instead, it is long-lasting in that it takes time for hikers to realize and feel the impact of their journeys on the Appalachian Trail.

The hiking community on the AT is undeniably varied. Some are there for the competitive aspect, bragging rights if you will; others are there for the spiritual aspect of connecting with God through their natural environment. No matter what their experience, hikers cannot deny that hiking the Appalachian Trail is also very much a social experience. Hikers like North Florida Swamp Donkey admit to becoming "more friendly and outgoing" after spending time with the hiking community. Drifter said he became a more patient person, too. He completed his first thru-hike at age thirty-three, a time when he believed he "became a better person all around, one easier to get along with, able to appreciate things," one who now sees the goodness in others. Interestingly, in light of the camaraderie or strong social and emotional bonds that form among long-distance hikers, social differentiation and hierarchies are still present on the Appalachian Trail just as they are in society. We focus on this aspect of the hiking community next.

5 ✒ THE APPALACHIAN TRAIL, AN ATOPIA?

Social Differentiation and Hierarchies among the Tribe

When referring to the great outdoors, we probably imagine a space that is open and accessible for all to enjoy regardless of race, gender, social class, occupation, age, ability, or sexual orientation, among other social divides. Most hikers describe the Appalachian Trail in this fashion. More specifically, a sentiment shared among long-distance hikers when speaking about the hiking community on the Appalachian Trail is the notion that everyone is equal. As simply stated by Obie, "Out there, out on the trail, it doesn't matter what you do. Everybody is the same. You want to stay fit, you prefer to stay dry, and you head north."

Shared economic position, or social class in the traditional sociological sense, is not what unites hikers, however; rather it is the embodied experience of hiking long distance. The following experience, recalled by Hustler, demonstrates the connection long-distance hikers share in spite of their perceived economic differences:

All of the hikers have this same connection here. You're all hiking to Maine. It's kind of cool because I was hiking with this multimillionaire last year who had a little bit better gear than we had obviously, and when he went into town he would stay in plush hotels and things like that. But, on the end of a rainy day, he would come into the shelter. One time it was fifteen-degree weather, not fifteen but it was really cold, pure hypothermia conditions. We hike into this shelter, and he's just as miserable as everybody else. It equals the field. In that way you feel connected to all the other hikers out here because you are experiencing everything. The experience doesn't really change whether you have money or not or what social class you're in. You're all one and all experiencing the exact same thing, the same pain, same everything, same weather conditions. It doesn't matter what kind of money you have or how good of shape you are in or what kind of gear you have. You're still suffering the same and going through the same experience.

Hikers perceive that the playing field is level because everyone faces the same physical and mental challenges or situations on the trail. Turbo recalled meeting a variety of people but said he did not see a common thread in terms of occupation. The only common thread he noticed among hikers was "dedication." In terms of hiking equipment or gear, he noted that "people have hiked the whole Appalachian Trail with a duffle bag or stuff they bought from Walmart." At the end of the day, "all they have to do is keep walking." On the trail, at least according to Branch, "prince and pauper are the same." Bramble argued that the trail itself is the great equalizer: "You get kids out here that are little delinquents, smoking marijuana or something like that. . . . Your elderly people, middle-aged people, doctors, lawyers, nurses, you name it. It doesn't matter what anybody does or has done in the past. Everybody is equal here. Everybody is equal. That's what's good about it." According to HeartFire, trail names play a part in the "leveling of everybody" on the Appalachian Trail: "We're all here under pseudonyms. Nobody knows who anybody is, but that's part of the leveling of everybody out here on the trail. You know, doctors, nurses, lawyers, judges, sanitation workers, blue collar nobodies, and people between jobs, we're all out here doing the same thing and we're all equal."

Like so many others mentioned in the previous chapters, Little Cubit said that interacting with other hikers was what she liked most about hiking the Appalachian Trail. She noticed, however, a lack of diversity within the hiking community:

There seems to be everybody from every walk of life, but it's not really true because we went to school in Charleston, South Carolina, and we saw, really saw, every walk of life there, but here you see the same stereotypes, the same archetype which is still okay. There are still a lot of educated people out in the woods. There are still a lot of interesting people with interesting backgrounds, but I just, I don't really see too much diversity. There aren't as many women as I would like. There aren't as many African Americans as I would like.

Little Cubit is correct. There is a homogeneous whiteness on the AT. More specifically, the typical long-distance hiker on the trail is a white, educated, middle-class male in his early twenties or late forties or older. It appears that social class—as well as race, gender, and age—although operating in the background, influences just who will hike the Appalachian Trail. It could be argued that while social differences are evident on the Appalachian Trail, they are often disregarded. These social cleavages of class, race, gender, and age are present by their very absence.

In the previous chapter, I explored the similarities between long-distance hiking and religious pilgrimage. You may recall from chapter 4 that once hikers remove themselves from society and their former lives to hike the Appalachian Trail, they enter the second stage of religious pilgrimage—the liminal stage—where transition takes place. Within this stage, there exists the potential for chaos as hikers enter a new realm devoid of structures to which they previously had been accustomed. At this point, rites of transition, such as the adoption of a trail name, can provide structure and assist hikers as they navigate this new environment and begin to establish meaningful relationships with strangers.

During the liminal stage, individuals are without status. In other words, no one occupies a particular rank or position. Individuals have no distinguishing characteristics that set them apart from each other. Everyone is the same. When this leveling process occurs for long-distance hikers on the Appalachian Trail, they come together as a community; they are all equal, and eventually they begin to think of themselves as one big traveling family.

This overarching theme of equality or "sameness" within the hiking community was brought up time and again by my interviewees, but this is not an entirely accurate description of relationships among hikers on the Appalachian Trail. In many cases, equality manifests itself, and in others the equality hikers speak of is less evident. A closer look at the language used by long-distance hikers when they refer to the hiking community reveals hierarchies and "judgments" similar to those found in mainstream society, only in a different form. This chapter builds on our understanding of relationships among long-distance hikers by paying careful attention to the boundaries hikers create as they distinguish themselves from other types of hikers. In what follows, I turn my attention to the social differences and hierarchies that emerge among hikers on the Appalachian Trail. Forms of tension are highlighted as hikers create and maintain both horizontal and vertical boundaries that reflect different roles or behaviors such as one's general approach to long-distance hiking. I end this chapter by focusing on one last characteristic of the hiking community—ways men and women create, sustain, and challenge gender difference through a variety of social practices and rituals as they negotiate this public space together.

DIVISIONS AMONG THE TRIBE

Once on the Appalachian Trail, it does not take long before a person realizes that there is an established hiker hierarchy, one that differentiates between types of hikers: thru-hikers, section hikers, weekend or overnight hikers, and day hikers. An implicit hiker hierarchy emerges that reflects a hiker's desires or motivations for being on the trail. Because of their investment in this recreational activity, thru-hikers are located at the top, followed by section hikers, weekend or overnight hikers, with day hikers coming in at the bottom. Is there tension between the types of hikers? Hatchet Jack said he guesses that "some thru-hikers don't like section hikers or other day hikers and such," maybe because of their perceived lack of commitment to hiking the trail all at once, but he had not personally found that to reflect reality on the trail itself. Thus, it appears as if these boundaries reflecting hiker types are not harshly drawn. Rather, they simply serve to distinguish hikers by type of use, setting long-distance hikers apart from other hikers who are on the Appalachian Trail short-term, for a day or weekend.

This implicit hiker hierarchy is not the only way hikers on the Appalachian Trail draw distinctions among one another. Hikers, regardless of hiker type, seem to fall into one of two general categories. In addition, long-distance hikers (thru-hikers and section hikers) are further stratified as a group themselves.

Chest-Thumpers and Dreamers

Generally speaking, there are two types of people on the Appalachian Trail, at least as described by members of the hiking community. Sunshine and Daydream referred to them as "chest-thumpers and dreamers." Slick distinguished between the two groups in a similar fashion. According to her:

> There's the people that seem to be like the really, really athletic-type who come out and they go. They go to the trail, and they get it done in four months and it's more of a get-to-the-end, accomplishment kind of thing. And, on the flip side, there's the people that are like, "Oh it's a waterfall," and sit by it for three hours and are like, "Oh well, I guess we're not doing a lot of miles today." That's the two main groups of people I've kind of noticed out here. And there's definitely more of the latter, I think.

Lady Mustard Seed also noticed "two calibers of hikers"—the dreamers or seekers out there and those "crazy, physical people who just want to test themselves and get those miles in as fast and hard as they can." At the same time, Lady Mustard Seed suggested that everyone who hikes the Appalachian Trail is a dreamer in some way, even the chest-thumpers. She believes "we've all been called out" for a reason, "even the really physical people that are out to just test themselves." Montreal, however, did not share Lady Mustard Seed's hopefulness or positivity. He tended to view the hiking community through a more critical lens, particularly those members who see their hikes as a competition. Kutsa, Montreal's wife, noted that although most hikers you come in contact with will tell you the hike is not a race, for many, in fact, it is: "We meet everybody since everybody passed us. So everybody tells us it's not a race but they all are, 'I did twenty today!' That's the first thing that they tell you. 'We did twenty' or 'We're doing a short day today. We're doing fifteen.' It's not a race but everybody makes sure to say their twenty or twenty-five or thirty." Kutsa admitted it would be nice to join the race. She would do so happily herself if she could but does not consider herself to be a fast hiker. Montreal added that some hikers will actually quit hiking the Appalachian Trail because of the competitive atmosphere, whether they are competing with others or themselves:

> A lot of people put pressure on themselves to finish the whole thing. It's a big challenge, two thousand miles, and you don't have medals at the end. A lot of

people have a hard time because after a while they say they are getting tired of the trail. Physically, it's hard. But they can blue blaze. A lot of time the trail goes up a mountain but you can take a side trail to go around. A lot of them won't do it and they really have a hard time because in real life you can, I think in society either you perform or there is this exit thing where you justify [your behavior and choices you make] to people—"Well, I was too tired"—but on the trail a lot of people don't give a shit. Take the side trail. But, they'll feel bad to do it. . . . They try to justify it but nobody gives a shit, you know, but they do it. "Well, I think I'm going to do a zero but the next day I'm going to fly." Well, that's all right. I think a lot of people, it's kind of unconscious, but they have a hard time because there is no exit door. Either you do it or you don't and it's up to you.

What Montreal seems to be suggesting is that in society, people are expected to perform; they should "just do it," to borrow a well-known slogan from Nike. Instead, people make excuses or feel the need to justify their choices and behavior to others, as well as to themselves; this is what he referred to as their "exit" in society. According to Montreal, these excuses or "exits" are not necessary on the Appalachian Trail, though some hikers feel inclined to make them.

Hiking the Appalachian Trail is no easy feat. People tend to "get bored" with the same scenery day after day, or "get tired of the trail" in sections where there are no views at all, or they may begin to feel as if they are no longer making progress. In the beginning, until they reach Damascus, Virginia, northbound hikers are clicking away the miles, as well as the states. Once they reach Virginia, however, some hikers experience what is commonly referred to as the Virginia blues. Hikers have made it roughly five hundred miles from Georgia to Virginia. For those who continue hiking, they will remain in Virginia for approximately the next five hundred and forty miles. The trail in Virginia alone makes up about one-fourth of the Appalachian Trail. Many hikers consider quitting at this point. To save face, they feel the need to justify their "exit" to other hikers, as well as to themselves, rather than simply performing or modifying their hike to continue the journey they set out to make.

Any justification or self-verification should not be necessary, as "hike your own hike" is a common mantra among long-distance hikers on the Appalachian Trail, meaning that hikers are free to hike the trail in a manner that satisfies them most. As Sunshine stated, "There are so many reasons to be out here, and as long as you get out of it what you wanted to then I think you're attaining your goal and fulfilling your experience." So, while the chest-thumpers may be hiking the trail "to prove something" or "to put the plaque next to their deer head," as Daydream suggested, Sunshine, his hiking partner, argued that this is their hike to make: "That's whatever they're groovin' on. . . . If the only thing that they want out of their experience is a plaque then good for them." To her, "they're attaining their goal," even if their goal is not fully aligned with the goals of other hikers who find themselves drawn to the trail.

Forms of Tension

Though "hike your own hike" is a common mantra among long-distance hikers, closer examination of the hiking community reveals that the freedom to do so is not embraced by all. In other words, not all long-distance hikers on the Appalachian Trail follow their own guidelines regarding the autonomy of someone to hike the trail as he or she desires. The implicit hiker hierarchy that differentiates between the different types of hikers further stratifies long-distance hikers on the basis of their approach to hiking, their point of entry, or the direction of their hike. They might be termed a purist, a white-blazer, blue-blazer, yellow-blazer, pink-blazer, flip-flopper, slackpacker, northbounder, or southbounder. These horizontal and vertical boundaries created by long-distance hikers may sometimes be harshly drawn.

On difficult days, "the trail community, the companionship, camaraderie, good friends" can help make or break a hiker's spirit, according to Taz. She said that the hiking community is great in that way. Taz, however, also recognized that the hiking community is just like the rest of the world, meaning that divisions and cliques form on the trail. So, even though there is a hiking community present that hikers identify with, there are also secondary groups that emerge among hikers. Kutsa and Montreal explained the hiking community on the Appalachian Trail this way:

MONTREAL: Sometimes the way they act on the trail is the same way they would act in society. Drifter, yesterday, I think he said at Partnership Shelter, it is funny because you have little cliques like gangs, and a lot of people think that because they are here, everything from the modern society is outside, which is not true. We have the same competition on the trail, the same social classes and type of people who look at each other a bit, you know. Some people have less education.

KUTSA: I think it's just on a different scale. Instead of "we're lawyers," when we're here it's on a different, either it's the clothes, the pace you're hiking, if you're with a cool group. If you're fast you want to keep up with the young fast group. If you're very slow or if you're overweight, "Maybe she won't make it." If you're slacking, if you're whatever, if you're not going straight and you're going to flip-flop, that's a different kind. Purists, blue-blazers, yellow-blazers. All that, I think, kind of puts it, it's a different language, but it's the same exact judgment almost I think.

As mentioned by Kutsa, long-distance hikers may slackpack (hike with only a small day pack), though this approach to hiking is not typically adopted or accepted by traditional thru-hikers or those who consider themselves "purists." Slackpacking most often occurs when hikers want to make big miles without the weight of their packs to slow them down. When slackpacking, hikers often leave their big pack with the person who drops them off and picks them up at the end of the day. This approach to hiking would not be acceptable to purists. Purists, also known as white-blazers, are hikers on the trail who believe the only way to thru-hike the Appalachian Trail is to hike every single white blaze, the official mark of the trail, and to do so with your pack on the entire trip. For Hobo Joe, being a purist "doesn't mean anything at all." In fact, he figures purists are "people who take it way too seriously" and in the end "don't have enough fun out here."

Though blue blazes typically indicate water sources, there are times when a hiker will come across a blue blaze signifying a scenic or less strenuous route. If this is the case, the scenic route is often noted in hiker handbooks. A blue-blazer then would be a long-distance hiker who substitutes a blue-blazed section of the trail between any two points on the AT. Yellow-blazers are individuals who walk on the roads near the trail, hitchhike, or drive the highway rather than hike the trail. Meeting a yellow-blazer is a rare occurrence unless you are also traveling the highways.

Commenting on these various categories, Taz said that while she enjoys the people on the trail, "not all of them are great," and further described some long-distance hikers as "bad eggs." I was curious as to how she determined who the "bad eggs" were:

It's interaction. They're very volatile. I mean they're mean, just downright mean. There are some that know how to do everything on the trail, and they're telling you how to do it right. And then they're others that just make fools of themselves. They kind of ruin the hiker reputation in towns. I think you know what I'm talking about. And then there are others that are mean to day hikers. It's like they're purists. Purists. That's another big thing. You're either a purist, a blue-blazer, a yellow-blazer, section hiker, whatever, like that. And some of the purists, not all I'll guarantee you that, but some of them are very, I mean once they learn that you are not following every single white blaze, it's like you're garbage so they treat you that way.

Being mindful not to include her with the "bad egg" purists, I asked whether she considered herself a purist and made a conscious effort to hike past every white blaze. Taz thought a minute and replied: "Not all of them. When I first found that whole idea, that purists are people I didn't want to be involved with, the next day I backtracked a mile and took the Kinsey Creek Trail, and I did the blue blaze so I wouldn't be a purist. It was great. It was like the greatest day I had in a couple of weeks." Whether or not anyone else knew she backtracked, Taz did not want to be associated with those who considered themselves purists. As a result, she decided to act in a way that would differentiate her hike, as well as her identity as a long-distance hiker, from theirs.

In addition to hikers' approaches to long-distance hiking, their point of entry on the trail and the direction of their hike are also used to differentiate them, though with less judgment. These boundaries, which are not harshly drawn, recognize a hiker's status or identity as a northbounder, southbounder, section hiker, thru-hiker, or flip-flopper. Flip-floppers are hikers who start at one terminus and hike to a certain point, get off the trail and jump to the other terminus and start hiking back to the place where they left the trail to fully complete their hike on the Appalachian Trail; whether or not one completes the entire trail, however, is irrelevant. If a hiker jumps around and switches direction, he or she is considered a flip-flopper. All of these individuals—flip-floppers, section hikers, thru-hikers, northbounders, and southbounders—could consider themselves white-blazers (that is, purists) or they could vary along this spectrum as blue-blazers, yellow-blazers, or even slackpackers, reflecting those value judgments that tend to be more harshly drawn among some members of the hiking community.

These descriptions of the hiking community on the Appalachian Trail allow us to conclude that membership, identity, and status as a long-distance hiker are, to a large extent, shaped by one's approach to hiking, as well as by one's point of entry and direction of one's hike. In many cases vertical boundaries created by long-distance hikers can be harshly drawn, as noted by Taz, Montreal, and Kutsa (that is, white-blazer, purist, section hiker, blue-blazer, slackpacker, yellow-blazer); this is not always the case, however. Horizontal boundaries that reflect where they started, or the direction of the hike, do not seem to be as harshly drawn among members of the hiking community on the Appalachian Trail.

The Practice of Pink-Blazing

Another type of hiker that may be encountered on the Appalachian Trail, though not previously mentioned, is a pink-blazer. Late one evening, as I was enjoying some trail magic and visiting with HeartFire, I recalled a comment Boone, another thru-hiker, had made about TV Ted, that TV Ted was pink-blazing. When I asked HeartFire what that meant, if she had heard the term, she quickly replied, "Oh that means he's chasing girls." What? Wait a minute. I had never heard that one before. White-blazers, blue-blazers, yellow-blazers, even an aqua-blazer (that is, traveling a section of the Appalachian Trail on water), but never a pink-blazer. As a result of this new term, I quickly realized that gender too has a way of surviving as hikers create and sustain gender hierarchies on the trail through a number of social practices and rituals.

Apparently TV Ted skipped one hundred miles of the Appalachian Trail and took a ride covering that stretch, getting back on at Front Royal, Virginia, where I first met him at the Jim and Molly Denton Shelter. What this means in terms of travel is that TV Ted essentially skipped Shenandoah National Park in northern Virginia or the one hundred miles of trail between Waynesboro and Front Royal. Because he was taking the easy way out, I just assumed Boone referred to TV Ted as a "pink-blazer" for taking rides and not hiking the whole trail. I honestly thought the more accurate term for TV Ted would have been yellow-blazer in this instance, even though he was not walking the highway. As it turns out, at least according to Boone, TV Ted was skipping around and taking rides from women so he could meet them.

This new term, pink-blazer, was beginning to make sense to me now as I recalled Sweet Sixteen telling me a funny story about her trail name in 2005:

Being older as I am, I'm kind of unique. Other hikers have read my registry journal, many young people. Then when you meet me they are, well, at first I met some young people, some young guys who said, "Oh, you're Sweet Sixteen? We were rushing to catch up with you." And that was embarrassing because I had never thought of that possibility. It was just supposed to be humorous, but then, they were very good about it and word got passed along I think.

Sweet Sixteen chose her own trail name to reflect the youthful spirit of the trail. To her, the trail was like the fountain of youth. As it turns out, the young men who were chasing Sweet Sixteen, who was actually in her early sixties, mistakenly thought they were chasing a sixteen-year-old female hiker.

These men, and others like TV Ted, are assumed to be in pursuit of women, enacting a presumed masculine tendency. The practice of pink-blazing may also give the impression that the Appalachian Trail is a context much like a club environment where men chase women; this relatively new term, however, could also refer to male hikers who pursue women for a variety of reasons, such as friendship, love, the desire for a female presence, or the wish for a familial bond shared with someone like a sister. For example, Bramble, the first hiker I ever interviewed, admitted that some guys do come to the Appalachian Trail hoping to meet someone, though he never used the term "pink-blazing." He also mentioned that once a guy realizes "the girl" is not interested, the relationship becomes more like that of brother and sister. Bramble was also quick to say that "not everybody comes out here to hook up. There's a community of people that float over that." That was refreshing to hear. I could not imagine people going to hike the Appalachian Trail to "hook up." After all, hikers go through what might be called "an uncivilizing process" in which they have only so many opportunities to bathe.

"Doing Gender" through Dress and Appearance

Gender—the social and cultural expectations and social practices associated with being men and women in society—is also reflected in the appearance and dress of long-distance hikers on the Appalachian Trail. For example, it is not unusual to see female hikers on the trail hiking in skirts. Gypsy Lulu, for instance, "brings a lot of color to the trail," which she said is reflected in the clothes she wears. She and her sister were both hiking in what she referred to as "snazzy hiking skirts" because they tend to dry a bit faster, or so she found. Another way femininity is emphasized through appearance is the practice of shaving one's legs in nearby streams, though not all women opt to do so. For some, the extra weight of a razor, even if minimal, is simply not worth it when every ounce carried matters.

Although women engage in behaviors and dress that reinforce femininity, they also present themselves and their bodies in ways that resist conventional standards of femininity. Spirit, for example, is "prim and proper at home" and bathes every day, "sometimes twice a day." She continued to describe her beauty regime at home and how that compares to life on the trail:

> I fix my hair. I don't wear it in public unless my hair is just perfect. I wear dresses most of the time. This is not, this is not how I would want it to be, but you learn, you learn to deal with it. I know last time when I went home after I'd hiked a while my kids told me "Mom, you've lost all modesty." You do, you lose, it's not that you lose it, but you learn that it wasn't that important. Life goes on and you can't fret about little things. I don't like being dirty all the time and stinkin' but you have to, you have to live like that.

Laughing, Spirit mentioned she could "go get in the cold creek" to wash off if she wanted, but at the end of a long day, who has the time or energy?

As Spirit indicated, life on the Appalachian Trail is different. Female hikers do not really care about the typical feminine displays found in mainstream society, though some hikers have to learn to make this adjustment for themselves. I recall my first backpacking trip on the AT in 1999. My hiking partner Big Pan asked me to lay out everything I was taking. Part of my "gear" included mascara and a small powder compact. When asked why in the world I would bring makeup on a hiking trip, my response was, "Well, we may go into town." I was quickly told to mail that home or throw the items away. There was indeed no reason for me to carry the added weight. Needless to say, I tossed the items, never giving them a second thought, nor did I ever find an occasion to need them.

On the Appalachian Trail it quickly becomes obvious that long-distance hikers do not feel as compelled to conform to conventional gender norms and practices, or at least they eventually come to realize this, as I did. Essentially, if you were a new hiker on the Appalachian Trail, you might think your entire world had been turned upside down. This is a place, a social world, where men sometimes wear skirts or sport kilts and women do not shave—although, in the interest of comfort, women have been known to shave their heads, as do men, to combat the heat and inconvenience of hiking during the peak of the summer. So, there is some gender bending or playfulness on the trail. In fact, quite a few men, younger men in most cases, even paint their fingernails and toenails in bright colors, a standard at Trail Days or so it seemed.

Though it may appear as if episodes of gender, or the ways hikers "do" or perform gender, are convenient or practical given life on the trail, there may not be as much license to play or experiment with gender as they initially thought, particularly when passing through local communities. When asked about such experiences, Bramble replied:

> I bought a kilt and I wear this kilt all the time . . . but some of the local communities through the trail aren't used to seeing men wearing kilts. They think they are just a dress or something. Some people don't know what a kilt is. Then when people approach you they expect you to be somebody different like a foreigner from a different country. And then when you don't sound exactly the way you are supposed to sound then they call the cops. Not that I am doing anything bad, it's just that people are concerned. I can tell you that in Bryson City, North Carolina, I went in to get resupplied. I went to the library, and just walking down the street someone saw me and called the police department and four cops approached me.

Bramble alluded to the importance of gender as a product of situated conduct. When he was off of the trail, others held him accountable for what they considered to be an inappropriate display of gender, or more specifically, masculinity. In other words, their expectations did not coincide with his appearance. To address this concern, Bramble bought a T-shirt that read "Special Forces" across the front to wear with his kilt as a way to reinforce his identity as a man, and perhaps his normalcy in the eyes of local community members he encountered off of the trail.

The Gendering of Trail Names and Hiker Interactions

The appearance and dress of long-distance hikers are not the only ways hikers perform gender on the Appalachian Trail. Gender is also evidenced in the giving and receiving of trail names. Vogue, for instance, was looking for a new T-shirt to wear on the trail. She ended up with an Appalachian Trail T-shirt and then became concerned about "wearing an AT T-shirt on the AT." She asked the opinions of the friends she was hiking with, who replied, "It doesn't matter; you're hiking, who cares?" Another female hiker told her she was being "too fashion conscious" and gave her the trail name Vogue. When I inquired as to what this name might suggest about her, Vogue laughingly admitted she hoped the name didn't suggest she was "too prissy out here" because she did not think she was at all. She did, however, like the sophistication the name implied. She also said that for those at home in Michigan who knew her, the name was appropriate.

Vogue was not the first trail name given to her, though. While hiking the previous year, she was given the trail name Rella, short for Cinderella: "One day, I was sitting in a pile of dirt, and I looked down and I was looking at my hands and my legs, and I was like 'Why am I so dirty?' and everybody else around me just started laughing and said, 'Really, you're in a pile of dirt!'" As a result of her concern over cleanliness, they started calling her Cinderella, which she did not really care for because it sounded "too princessy." When the opportunity presented itself to take a new trail name the following year, Vogue gladly accepted.

When considering the various trail names of male and female hikers, I noticed that compared to males, female hikers were more likely to have the word "little" as part of their trail names, such as Little One, Little Feet, and Little Cubit. I did not encounter a man with such a distinction. Male hikers, on the other hand, tended to have trail names like Big Pan and Mr. Pink. Other women had trail names that reflected their spirituality or youth, like Graceful, Spirit, and Sweet Sixteen, whereas male names reflected power, strength, or speed, as in Hatchet Jack, Turbo, Hustler, and Chainsaw.

Though gender may be influential in the giving and receiving of trail names, long-distance hikers may also choose a trail name that is symbolic or reflective of gender as well, like married couple Lady Mustard Seed and North Florida Swamp Donkey. When deciding on a trail name, North Florida Swamp Donkey wanted to give a tribute to his home region, Tallahassee, Florida, hence the portion North Florida Swamp. Donkey, he laughingly admitted, "comes from just being, basically, my wife's pack animal." According to him, his wife gave him that part of his name, after deciding against

Burro. Swamp Donkey reflected on what these two names, North Florida Swamp Donkey and Lady Mustard Seed, suggested about them as a couple:

> [North Florida Swamp Donkey] kind of compliments my wife's name, which is [Lady] Mustard Seed—the more thoughtful. It's got the biblical connotations. Mine I think shows that I have a little more fun, am a little more loose, and that's kind of how we are. We have a serious side, and we have a side that likes to get crazy, drink some beers. It's good because when we meet people, they either attach to her name or my name, so it's kind of worked out cool like that.

Generally speaking, a man's trail name tends to reinforce conventional notions of masculinity. Donkey, for example, implies that Swamp Donkey is stronger or more physically fit than his wife, hence the reason he is her pack animal. At the same time, her trail name, Lady Mustard Seed, also emphasizes traditional notions of femininity. She is, after all, "the more thoughtful" of the two, the "lady." Their trail names might even imply that she is in control of her behaviors, while he can unleash his inner animal and "get crazy," something a "lady" would not dare do herself as she is more refined. One thing I did notice, in terms of emotional labor, is that the more time women spend on the trail hiking, the less maternal or nurturing they become. Below is a description of an event I witnessed in May 2007 near Deer Lick Shelter, fifteen miles south of Pennsylvania:

> Everybody is in pain out here. Hikers often say you've got to learn to be comfortable being uncomfortable. If you feel good, something's wrong. So why must others complain!! I met a couple of hikers taking a break along the trail today. The female hiker was saying to her male hiking partner that he needed to suck it up and quit whining. The look on his face was priceless. I tried not to smile. She was right. His pain is not unique. All he has to do is leave. Too true! We don't need the negativity out here. It's tough enough.

In this excerpt from my fieldnotes, gender is both reinforced and contested as hikers interact with one another when dealing with the aches and pains of hiking long distance. This interaction illustrates how women may subvert gender while men reaffirm gender simultaneously. Female hikers tend to be less maternal and nurturing toward others than would be presumed, given expectations concerning "appropriate" gendered behavior for women. Male hikers, on the other hand, are taken aback and hold women accountable for what they consider to be an "inappropriate" display of gendered behavior. Recall the astonishment and surprise on the male hiker's face when his partner did not console him in his time of need.

Interestingly, hikers like Lady Mustard Seed and Swamp Donkey, whose relationships existed before their hike of the Appalachian Trail, seemed to bring an understood division of labor with them. For example, Sunshine mentioned that her fiancé, Daydream, was "always wanting to help and wanting to take more weight out of my pack," which was, at times, frustrating for her because she wanted to be more independent; she "is not a wimpy little girl." Sunshine knew that is not why Daydream was offering his assistance but still wanted to be able to do for herself. Since they were a couple, I asked if they shared the daily chores at camp equally or if there was some preexisting gendered division of labor:

DAYDREAM: I always cook, and she always cleans. That's how it was at home.
SUNSHINE: Yeah, I think we just transferred the routine that we had off the trail to the trail, and it's been working pretty well for us so far.

Daydream went on to say that they were both "extremely flexible" and simply do whatever needs to be done at the time. My hiking partner and I are the same way, though he typically gathers firewood when we first arrive at camp, and I seem to be the one putting up the tent or setting up in a shelter, as the case may be. I suppose you could consider him "the gatherer" and me "the homemaker," but we do not view the division of labor this way. We both share equally in the cooking and cleaning, as well as collecting and purifying water and packing up in the mornings. We also share equally in chores like laundry and shopping when in town to resupply.

Sharing chores and supplies is a bit easier when you have a second person, as Hazy Sonic, a thirty-year-old married man from Indiana, noted. Rather than carrying everything yourself, "you can divide up the weight." Plus, it helps on occasions when one person may have blisters or other foot problems. The other person can always take on a little more weight. Hazy Sonic humorously suggested, though, that when his wife, Firefly, is hiking a little too fast, he can always add a little weight to her pack when she is not looking in order to slow her down.

Although I encountered a few married couples on the Appalachian Trail, including a newly married couple thru-hiking for their honeymoon, married couples are the exception rather than the rule. As I mentioned earlier, the overwhelming majority of long-distance hikers on the AT are young, single, white men who have just finished high school or college and are uncertain where life is going to take them, or alternatively, men in their midforties and older. This aspect, the large number of single men, was one dynamic that North Florida Swamp Donkey did not particularly care for: "There's like a lot of testosterone going on because the majority is single guys out here. And the people that hike the Appalachian Trail, I'd say a majority of them, have hiking experience . . . and it can be kind of intimidating. They can kind of group up. They can be kind of cliquey." Maybe these were some of the "chest-thumpers," to borrow from Daydream. At the same time, North Florida Swamp Donkey acknowledged that his initial impression of the men could simply be from his and his wife's perspective. Regardless, they did not enjoy feeling intimidated or pressured to compete. As it turns out, they left the trail for a few days, skipped ahead, and found other hikers who were more welcoming and supportive.

In terms of cooking, there is also a gendering of food preparation, although not in the way one might assume. On the Appalachian Trail, cooking becomes a homosocial event for men. In other words, in mainstream society we typically think of cooking and sharing recipes as a woman-centered activity. On the trail, however, Spirit and Swinging Jane found themselves impressed with the men:

SPIRIT: I'm impressed with the guys on the trail. I mean they're really culinary cooks on here. For me, I'm just really simple. I would rather just fix something warm to get in my body and be in my sleeping bag.

SWINGING JANE: That's true, I've watched them.

SPIRIT: They come in and they all pitch in, if there's a group of them, they add to the pot.

SWINGING JANE: A lot of cooperation goes on.

SPIRIT: Yeah, and they love to brag about what they're cooking. And it smells good. Of course, I guess they carry a lot more stuff than we do. I mean most of the young people are carrying all of this junk food and stuff, but the guys, most of the guys have stuff they mix together and cook and try. I'm really impressed with the guys on here.

From this dialogue between Spirit and Swinging Jane, it appears as if male hikers both reinforce and subvert conventional gender norms and practices associated with food preparation while on the trail. To be sure, outdoor cooking—grilling—has long been viewed as men's domain. Thus, moving cooking outdoors removes the potential "stigma" of emasculation for an activity that, when performed indoors, is commonly viewed more as women's work.

Swinging Jane continued to suggest that being on the Appalachian Trail is also a learning experience for men, just as it would be for women or anyone backpacking for the first time. Funny enough, male hikers appear to be more knowledgeable, or at least want to be perceived as being more knowledgeable about long-distance hiking and camp rituals. When camping with T-Mac and Turbo one evening, my hiking partner and I noticed something about how T-Mac took care of the campfire. To increase the flame, he would crouch down really close to the fire and put his index fingers and thumbs together to make a diamond and blow. We asked what he was doing and he said it was the "diamond dragon." T-Mac seemed to take ownership of this technique and said this method was much better for starting a fire because your breath would be concentrated and go directly to the fire rather than being dispersed into the air. It was only a few moments later when Turbo told T-Mac that he should not be taking credit for such an "awesome technique." As it turns out, Turbo shared with us that T-Mac learned this new technique for tending fire from a female hiker a few days earlier, something this "true outdoorsman" failed to mention.

To be sure, the physical features and difficulty of the Appalachian Trail—its rugged terrain or sometimes openness—can and do affect how long-distance hikers experience and perform gender on the trail. Conventional gender roles are evidenced and reinforced on the trail as men initially find themselves taking on more of a protector role when hiking with women. Male hikers may presume women are weaker, given their smaller frame and perceived vulnerabilities, and as a result may not be able to negotiate this space successfully. As Bramble, a return thru-hiker, noted: "The females are really protected out on the trail, and I wish that other females would realize that [the trail] is a safe environment. I wish that more females would get involved in hiking this journey because it is not all about fear, because people hike in groups . . . the community itself takes care of each other." Hatchet Jack noticed that while many female hikers may start out alone, they often make friendships or associations with others, male and female, as do the majority of long-distance hikers regardless of gender. Even when two or more female hikers are hiking together, however, men may still feel a need to offer protection and support, as Bramble did:

> Yeah, like those two females, they were hiking by themselves and I am going the same way. I could do twenty-five to thirty miles a day if I wanted to, but I guess out here, even as a man, it makes you feel good to look after someone. They're going the same way I'm going and there is no reason for me to go faster or anything. And it makes me feel good, being a hiker, that I know I am going to help them see their journey along the way. That is how it is out here. Everybody looks out for each other.

In Bramble's case, though, he could have easily been engaged in this masculine behavior, helping and looking out for the two women, more for himself than for them. For Bramble, his most challenging experience while hiking the Appalachian Trail was not the physical aspect but being alone and being single. He was raised by women most of his life, had been married for eight years, and prior to his hike had ended a three-year relationship. By taking on the role of protector in this rugged environment, Bramble was able to reaffirm his masculinity and status as a man.

Though often protected, most female hikers do feel safe on the trail, counter to what some might assume. HeartFire belongs to a women-only hikers group online, and the group often talks about safety when hiking alone, so she felt prepared. She did mention, however, that women on the trail worry about "the rape issue," though there have rarely been any problems reported. Most hikers are not worried in the woods and are actually more alert when going into town to resupply or when the trail crosses a local road or highway, particularly if there is a parking area nearby. Heart-Fire described one such occasion that made her feel a little uneasy:

> There's only one time when I came across somebody who was really scary on the trail and that was near Dragon's Tooth last year. And this was a guy who had an old army knapsack, a big buck knife that he was playing with, wearing jeans. One of them was torn down the back of his leg and he had on cotton thermals underneath it. And there were the blue blazes to the Dragon's Tooth and he wanted to know where the water was. And I said, "I think it's down by

the parking lot," because I didn't think there was water up there. He scared me. Fortunately, I knew there were a lot of other hikers around, male hikers, so I wasn't too worried about it. But the thing is not to be near road crossings on the weekends. But in the woods, I feel safe. I feel fine.

Most long-distance hikers, like HeartFire, feel safer in the woods than in town or near a road crossing. This feeling of security comes from the tight-knit relationships that form among members of the hiking community on the Appalachian Trail. Camaraderie and companionship are essential if long-distance hikers are to negotiate this shared space successfully. Of course, HeartFire does mention that she worried a little less because there were male hikers around. So, men often do take on a protector role, and women seem to depend on men under certain circumstances, reaffirming conventional gender norms on the trail.

For many hikers, the feeling that they need to protect or need protecting begins long before they take their first step on the Appalachian Trail. Slick, for example, had it "so ingrained" into her head before she left that as a female she would not be able to make it in the woods on her own: "Everyone's first response was, 'You're a girl. You can't go out there by yourself.' And I had that so ingrained in my head that I was like, 'I can't be out here by myself. My guys can't leave me.'" Initially, Slick started out with three others, all men she had met at Springer. She admitted they had become "her security blanket" in a way. Slick noticed how at the start, the four of them fell into gendered roles. The male hikers would always make the fire and offer to hang her bear bag each night, both of which she did not particularly mind them doing. When they left the trail after one was injured, Slick admitted she was a bit anxious, as well as angry, because she now had to fend for herself alone in the woods. Slick walked the anger off after the first hour or so and realized that being independent and being able to focus solely on herself was a nice change of pace. As a result, Slick became empowered and felt stronger and more independent as a young woman hiking alone in the woods.

While the ethic of self-reliance in this context is empowering for female hikers, the vast majority still do not hike alone. Little Cubit, for example, was hiking with her boyfriend because she tends to be "a trusting soul." Though she had not felt particularly uncomfortable, Little Cubit did say that if she were not with her boyfriend, she would have brought a dog along for the hike. In fact, the presence of hiking dogs on the trail is slowly becoming a rule rather than an exception, for both male and female hikers (see fig. 10).

Gender and the Negotiation of Space

Hiker interactions also involve the negotiation of space in this unpredictable and, in many cases, unfamiliar environment. In other words, there are many sites and spaces on and near the Appalachian Trail that male and female hikers must negotiate, especially when dealing with hygiene issues. For example, on the trail there are no sex-assigned bathrooms as there are in modern society, particularly in public places. There is no sign reading "men" or "women" posted anywhere on the trail itself. Everyone uses the same privy (outhouse), as they would at home—that is, of course, if there is a privy to be used at all. In fact, one complaint of long-distance hikers is that there are simply not enough privies along the trail in Tennessee. In the

10. New friends, Swinging Jane and Spirit, with Swinging Jane's hiking companion, 2005. Photograph by author.

absence of privies, men simply turn to the nearest tree, for the most part going unnoticed. This option is not as practical for women. To relieve themselves they often leave their packs by the trail and hunt for a large tree.

There are other sites that men and women inhabit more equally, where they resist gender out of necessity, such as at shelters and hostels. As Heart-Fire noted, "I've been at shelters where I've been the only woman . . . but I've been in shelters where there were about nine or ten women and two men." Sleeping arrangements are on a first-come, first-served basis. You never really know who you might end up sharing sleeping space with unless you are hiking with a particular group or at the same pace as others. There are many occasions when I have been the lone female hiker in a shelter or hostel. This seemed to happen, more often than not, the farther north I hiked, or when I was section hiking a northern part of the trail, as there are fewer thru-hikers in this area, given the percentage of those who exit.

On the trail most hikers do not really bathe. There may be opportunities to wash off in a stream, but the feeling of cleanliness is only temporary as hikers work up a sweat the following day, if not in a matter of minutes. One option for doing away with the sweat of the sun is to night hike, which some hikers do during the peak of the summer, sleeping during the day and hiking at night. Sometimes people hike in one set of clothes and then change upon arriving at the shelter or camping area for the night. On these occasions, hikers are respectful of one another's privacy to change. As Swinging Jane noted, "The men are really respectful of the ladies out here." Spirit suggested that this is because hikers are simply "in awe of one another."

While sleeping arrangements and bathing on the trail are, for the most part, non-issues for hikers, gender difference is often reinforced in local communities and hostels. For example, the Twelve Tribes Community, a religious community in Rutland, Vermont, separated hikers by gender into men's and women's bunkrooms. This arrangement applied to everyone, regardless of marital status. As a result, gender can be understood as a property of situated conduct. In other words, context—trail life or town—matters in terms of how we "do gender." I would venture that adherence to expected gendered behaviors and practices matters less on the Appalachian Trail than it does in mainstream society—or does it? Along with packs and tents, long-distance hikers carry cultural values and social practices through which gender differences learned in everyday life are transposed and affirmed. As is the case in other social venues, however, gender on the Appalachian Trail is subject to negotiation and, at times, subversion.

RECONFIGURATIONS AMONG THE TRIBE

Though long-distance hikers may give the impression that the hiking community is a model society, a social world in which everything is perfect and everyone gets along, the Appalachian Trail should not be characterized as a utopia where social differentiation or hierarchies do not exist. Just as individuals form cliques in society, social groupings are present on the Appalachian Trail, even if organized around a recreational activity as opposed to an economic class. In fact, close examination of the language used by long-distance hikers in referencing themselves and others reveals the structure of this multilayered leisure subculture.

Put succinctly, the social world of long-distance hikers is structured as well as individualized and competitive. Forms of stratification created by members of the hiking community on the Appalachian Trail are shaped simultaneously by use patterns, an individual's approach to hiking, the hiker's point of entry, and the direction of the hike. These forms of stratification are further overlaid by class, race, gender, and age. In the absence of clearly defined social norms, long-distance hikers import key aspects of gender onto the Appalachian Trail. Specifically, long-distance hiking illuminates how gender is created, sustained, and at times challenged in liminal social venues.

As a microcosm of the broader social world, long-distance hiking highlights various social distinctions, as well as the deeply engendered character of American culture. In other words, long-distance hikers on the Appalachian Trail seem to have one foot inside the American cultural mainstream and one foot outside of it.

6 ↗ HIKE YOUR OWN HIKE

What the Hiking Subculture Tells Us about American Society

Over the course of this study of hikers and community on the Appalachian Trail, we have discovered a great deal. Ethnographic fieldwork and in-depth interviews of hikers allowed them to articulate their lived experiences inside this leisure subculture, and allowed us to more thoroughly understand and evaluate the nature and extent of their belonging to one another and to the Appalachian Trail. In chapter 1, I outlined a series of questions facing scholars, as well as those in charge of managing natural resource–based recreational settings. One of those questions was How do we understand the long-distance hiking community in terms of the sociality and social practices of its members?

Recognizing that subcultures are best conceptualized as products of social interaction (Gelder 2007), I aimed to focus specifically on long-distance hikers' relationships and social practices on the trail. Compared to other hikers, long-distance hikers along the trail live mostly in isolation, with their own ways of acting, talking, and thinking; their own vocabulary; their own activities and interests; their own conception of what is significant in life; and to a certain extent their own scheme of life. In other words, long-distance hikers on the Appalachian Trail create a distinct social world, which is imperative if the hiking community is to be considered a subculture. Earlier in the volume I discussed how long-distance hikers can be identified by a range of attributes that include their behavior, style of dress, language, and diet, in comparison with those of "normal" populations. For example, long-distance hikers place an unreasonable amount of trust in strangers, both on and off the trail. It is common for hikers to accept rides from strangers and even to be welcomed into a stranger's home, if only for a shower or home-cooked meal. While most people tend to watch their caloric intake, long-distance hikers are rarely, if ever, concerned as they engage in excessive food consumption on nearly every occasion that presents itself, whether in towns or during "hiker feeds" along the trail. Although hikers might be viewed as lacking self-control with respect to food, generally the overwhelming majority of them are motivated and extremely self-disciplined. They continue hiking day after day in spite of unpredictable weather or the pain and physical discomfort that becomes commonplace. In other words, a typical long-distance hiker learns to be comfortable with discomfort.

Long-distance hikers can also be identified by an uncivilized or impoverished appearance, which often leads nonhikers to the conclusion that hikers are lazy and unproductive. Of course, many long-distance hikers are aware of this negative stereotype and confront it directly. Some long-distance hikers may be hiking for a cause, or they may take their work with them on the trail; they may view their hike as an alternative to legitimate work, or they may equate the physical and mental aspects of long-distance hiking as work. Other long-distance hikers, however, think of the Appalachian Trail as the antithesis of work and find themselves hiking because they were unhappy with their job situations. Still others are spiritually motivated and view their hike as a religious pilgrimage of sorts, rites of passage included. They too are seeking refuge in the wilderness, away from societal distractions or "negatives" (such as media influence, consumerism, materialism, and stresses of work and family) that do not allow them the time to focus on themselves, their families, or their relationship with God as they understand it. Regardless of their reasons for hiking, the unstructured features associated with long-distance hiking—such as rootlessness, spontaneity, and living outside structured realms of work, production, and property ownership—are invested with positive rather than negative values by members of this leisure subculture.

Though long-distance hikers appear to resist larger societal structures, both bureaucratic and social, the long-distance hiking community is not without its own organizing structure. In the last chapter, I examined the hiker hierarchy of thru-hiker, section hiker, weekend or overnight hiker, and day hiker on the Appalachian Trail. I also found that long-distance hikers (both section and thru-hikers) are further stratified as a group, with boundaries reflecting each one's approach to hiking long distance (for example, subgroups include purists, white-blazers, blue-blazers, yellow-blazers, pink-blazers, flip-floppers, slackpackers, and northbounders and southbounders). I ended the chapter by highlighting the complex or contradictory character of gender as hikers create, sustain, and challenge gender difference through a variety of social practices and rituals. In spite of all these differences, or the widely held mantra of "hike your own hike," the majority of long-distance hikers on the Appalachian Trail consider themselves to be part of one large hiking community or "traveling family" united through their participation in a particular recreational activity and the unique situations encountered while hiking the trail. Of course, this feeling of belonging, of family, can be temporary or permanent, depending on who is asked. In any event, this feeling is real for long-distance hikers on the Appalachian Trail.

In addition to broadening the focus of research into leisure subcultures and subcultural identities that form around specific places, we must also broaden conceptions of management policies aimed at providing visitors with desired recreational experiences. Currently, there are perceived inconsistencies regarding the physical, social, and managerial settings associated with the Appalachian Trail, particularly within the Great Smoky Mountains National Park. Hikers' frustrations with this portion of the trail (shelter reservations are too regulated; policies do not take the thru-hiker experience into account; and the time for hiking through the park is too limited) were detailed in chapter 2 and came largely from those who identified themselves as thru-hikers. Many felt their desired recreational experiences, including time for contemplation, the flexibility to stay longer in shelters, the impact of weather on their stay, and the various sleeping options, were not being met by those in charge of managing this particular section of the trail. If the goal, as defined by the U.S. Forest Service (1982), is to provide recreationists with their desired experiences, then recreation resource managers may need to revisit the amount and type of restrictions placed on hikers' actions while traveling the 71 miles through the Great Smoky Mountains National Park.

One way to begin addressing these perceived inconsistencies would be to modify existing use surveys designed to capture and enhance the visitor experience. For example, in their comprehensive survey on use and users of the Appalachian Trail, Manning and colleagues (2000) included statements such as "I enjoy hiking along the Appalachian Trail more than any other trail" or "Hiking here is more important than hiking any other place." Including a prompt to answer why would be helpful in understanding a hiker's reasons for choosing the Appalachian Trail over other hiking trails, as well as the reasons individuals continue to return. It would also be helpful on the survey to distinguish between hiking and long-distance hiking. As may be recalled from chapter 1, I was interested in exploring how the leisure activities of hiking and long-distance hiking or backpacking differ. Hiking implies a short-term activity, whereas long-distance hiking suggests spending multiple days, weeks, and or months on a hiking trail, which often leads to stronger feelings of attachment to recreational settings. To be sure, managing recreational areas for those who develop an emotional bond with a leisure setting like the Appalachian Trail is simply not as clear for those in charge of managing the area for a particular activity such as hiking would be. This difficulty arises in part because recreationists who use public lands often do so with conflicting needs and goals in mind, even if they are part of the same hiking community. For example, the motives of some long-distance hikers are instrumental, that is, they hike for the spiritual experience or for the challenge. The motives of others, however, are value-laden, that is, they see hiking as an expression of their identity. At any rate, on the basis of what was shared with me, it does not appear as if the motivations and experiences of long-distance hikers are fully taken into consideration by the National Park Service, the agency responsible for the 71-mile section of trail through Great Smoky Mountains National Park.

In addition, sites and places frequented by long-distance hikers, as well as a familiarity with hiker traditions, trail names, trail magic, and trail journals, could be included on use surveys to determine the extent to which hikers are immersed in the larger hiking community on the Appalachian Trail. When attitudes, beliefs, feelings, and values that long-distance hikers attach to the Appalachian Trail are known and understood, those in charge of making decisions can better manage the recreational setting for the social and emotional bonds, and the desired experiences of all recreationists, rather than focusing on a particular activity, such as hiking, or type of user who most frequents the area, such as day hikers. This discussion leads me to my last inquiry: What impact do recreational settings have in the formation of leisure subcultures and subcultural identities, and how does the long-distance hiking subculture sustain itself in the absence of continued face-to-face interaction?

THE SIGNIFICANCE OF PLACE

Sociologists, when speaking of the development of the self, focus on a socially situated self that is constructed in relation to significant others. Largely missing is the notion that we are place-situated beings, that we form identities in relation to significant places. In contemporary society, our identities are less clearly defined given the multiple roles we occupy and are creatively fashioned by a patchwork of relationships with family, friends, colleagues, and others. Now, this patchwork can also include meaningful places to which we become attached. Long-distance hikers experience this attachment when they leave the Appalachian Trail and rejoin society, bringing with them new identities formed on the trail, which now must unite, or possibly compete, with old ones left behind.

Of course, these newly formed identities may be temporary, though they seem to be permanent for the overwhelming majority of hikers interviewed. Once a hiker is back home, a trail identity seems to be less salient, although no less important to the hiker's overall self-concept. Trail identities are more easily activated when people are actually hiking the trail, particularly in situations where hikers leave the trail to resupply in towns. Several long-distance hikers mentioned feeling more at home and more comfortable in the woods and on the trail than they felt in towns. Some even described feeling like an "alien" and longing to get back to the trail, or feeling an itch to retreat back to the woods.

For long-distance hikers, the Appalachian Trail is a "storied" place where the power of place unfolds in the stories hikers share about their trail experiences. These stories are often filled with intense emotion, as hikers speak about their attachment to the natural environment of the trail. Kutsa told the following story:

It rained, and after the rain it cleared and it was about five o'clock in the afternoon and it was toward the end of the hike, so I had done by that time maybe seventeen miles. So I hiked and suddenly I stopped. I was alone. And the weirdest thing happened to me. I looked around and the light in the afternoon it just made this orange beautiful light. And there were all of these drops hanging on the leaves and everything was like gold around. And I stood and my blood was going so fast in my body that I could feel every inch of my body, I could feel the skin, everything, and I stood there and then I had this rush, just a rush of emotions. I started crying and then I started laughing. I just couldn't stop. It was just this extreme rush. And then I felt in love. Like you know how you feel with someone when you suddenly fall in love, like these butterflies with you when you see someone? I felt it, and it was not with someone. It was real love with nothing. I just felt this with no someone there. Not anyone in mind or anything. It was this moment of, I've never felt this before. Never, never, never. I don't really tell it to a lot of people. I actually never told it to anybody off the trail. Just for a few people, maybe, very close to me on the trail. And after that I never had it again. Never. It was this kind of weird thing, and I could, for the first few months, I could go back to that experience and it really helped me. I would go up mountains with no problem. I could kind of re-create, but it was something that for the rest of my life I would kind of search for. This kind of moment because it was just amazing. My hair on my hands stood for a few days after. It was so powerful.

Many long-distance hikers on the Appalachian Trail experience something authentic, like Kutsa did, due to the embodied nature of long-distance hiking. In fact, many stories shared by long-distance hikers revolve around their bodies, from the initial hiker's hobble to the evolution of trail legs, from pain and blisters due to rocky terrain, from excessive amounts of eating and extreme weight loss, to the emotional highs and lows related to unpredictable weather patterns. The extended period of time spent hiking the trail, and sharing similar stories with fellow long-distance hikers, strengthens the social and emotional ties hikers attach to this place and to the hiking community. Place does indeed matter to those who develop a relationship with the Appalachian Trail. Montreal summed this up nicely:

Yeah, like the guy [Nimblewill Nomad] who wrote *Ten Million Steps*, he's doing conferences and people ask him why do you go back on the trail, and he said that that's a question he cannot answer. You feel it, your body feels it, you just cannot say it in words. . . . You ask a lot of two-timers why do they come back and they will say nature or this or that, but it's something else that a lot of times you cannot express, this thing that you feel.

As mentioned throughout this book, many long-distance hikers, like Nimblewill Nomad of *Ten Million Steps*, come back to the Appalachian Trail time and again. A common thread shared by those who return is a feeling or a longing that they find difficult to express. Their trail identity seems to reflect a feeling of deep connection to the physical and natural environment of the trail itself, something difficult to explain unless one has experienced it firsthand. For some hikers, this feeling or trail identity may be fleeting, only activated when conversing with fellow long-distance hikers at events like Trail Days. For others, a trail identity is more prominent, leading them to return to the Appalachian Trail because they feel "alien" anywhere else. The trail has become their life.

As I mentioned in chapter 1, much of the leisure research on the Appalachian Trail has focused primarily on the activity of hiking as opposed to long-distance hiking or backpacking. While long-distance hiking includes the physical act of hiking, it also includes camping and backpacking over an extended period of time. As a result, long-distance hikers develop stronger feelings of attachment to the trails they are hiking and to the hiking community. What I offer here with respect to leisure subcultures is a marriage of place and activity in the formation of a long-distance hiking subculture. In other words, not only does the Appalachian Trail bind members of the subculture together, but so does the extended activity of long-distance hiking. So, given the variety of meanings associated with the Appalachian Trail, the number of people who hike with all of their unique characteristics, and the fact that the hiking community is more of a "traveling family," to borrow from Gus, how is it possible for a long-distance hiking subculture to sustain itself?

(SUSTAINING) A SUBCULTURE OF PLACE

Generally speaking, subcultures fall into two categories: those characterized by diffuseness and those characterized by coherence. Ken Gelder's subcultural perspective recognizes both fluid and persistent membership within subcultures; he does not, however, specifically address the processes through which a subculture sustains itself. Usually members of a subculture engage in face-to-face interaction, which helps transmit and sustain the culture, but this is not the case for long-distance hikers, who often are not in direct contact with one another due to the nature of this long-term recreational activity. Although relationships among long-distance hikers are likened to familial bonds or those formed in the military, the hiking community on the Appalachian Trail is in a constant state of flux as hikers move on and off the trail. Because the community is constantly evolving, the amount of face-to-face interaction a hiker has with other members of the hiking community varies, depending on the direction a person is hiking, as well as their point of entry. So, how does the long-distance hiking subculture on the Appalachian Trail sustain itself? It appears as if, rather than depending primarily on face-to-face interaction, a place referent mediates, bringing cohesion and solidarity to members of this leisure subculture.

According to Griswold (2008), flows of information are not automatic but must be channeled and mediated. In the absence of formal institutions, the hiker subculture is transmitted and sustained through electronic and popular media such as the Appalachian Trail Conservancy website, the magazine *A.T. Journeys*, various handbooks and guidebooks published for hiking the AT, hiker journals accessible through electronic media, Bill Bryson's *A Walk in the Woods*, and the numerous hiker memoirs, all of which reference the Appalachian Trail. Persons interested in hiking the trail need only type such terms as "thru-hiking" or "Appalachian Trail" into a search engine to be led to numerous hiker webpages, trail journals, or other sites (for example, whiteblaze.net) where people share stories about their experiences and offer advice on hiking the trail. There are also Facebook pages that one can "like" to learn more about the AT such as Appalachian Trials.

Also, cultural intermediaries such as trail angels, local community members, and religious groups are key variables that help transmit and sustain the long-distance hiking subculture on the AT. Most of these individuals, including former thru-hikers, come back year after year to give trail magic to hikers or to assist them in other ways. Through traditions such as these, stories are told and new memories made. The stories told and experiences shared by these cultural intermediaries also connect the current year's hikers to those of previous years, leading those new to the trail to feel as if they are part of a larger community, although they've never met in person. Encounters like these can activate a long-distance hiker identity as hikers on the Appalachian Trail begin to recognize who they are in reference to other groups such as nonhikers and trail angels. For example, a person's first interaction with a trail angel offering him trail magic could be all it takes to trigger an awareness of himself as a member of the hiking community.

In the absence of continued face-to-face interaction, the hiking subculture on the Appalachian Trail is also transmitted by hikers themselves, past and present, interacting and communicating with one another through established symbols, meanings, and behavioral norms that serve to bind the group together. For example, through participation in this recreational activity, the ritual of pilgrimage, the giving and receiving of trail names and trail magic, as well as the shared experiences of sacrifice and perseverance, long-distance hikers become connected as a group. At the same time, there are further distinctions among members of this group. These subtle differences are a reflection of negotiated roles and outcomes within the hiking community because not everyone will hike the Appalachian Trail in the same way or for the same reasons. Most long-distance hikers recognize and appreciate the freedom to hike the trail as each sees fit. As Turbo stated in chapter 5, "All you have to do is keep walking." In the end, for members of this multilayered leisure subculture, the AT is a special, symbolic place that unites them. Viewing the hiking community on the Appalachian Trail as a microcosm of the broader social world, I offer some final insights on what the long-distance hiking subculture reveals about American society and our relationships with the natural environment, as well as what part meaningful places play in shaping our identities, our lives, and our relationships with others.

THE POLITICS OF PLACE

My examination of the long-distance hiking subculture, as well as identity construction, is situated within the nature–society debate. Two major perspectives in this debate illuminate the relationship between humans and natural environments: essentialism and social constructionism (Greider and Garkovich 1994; Minteer 2001). Essentialists adopt the view that nature and the environment exist outside us and that there is a transcendental or superior quality to nature beyond common thought or experience. Several suggestions are offered as to why individuals may view nature as "Other," some of which have been articulated by long-distance hikers: the influence of science and technology, a disenchantment with the world, or a feeling that we, as individuals, have lost touch with our natural selves (Nordquist 2006).

Constructionists, on the other hand, suggest that nature and the environment are evolving social constructs whose origins are found within society. From this perspective, nature is viewed as both a social and a material expression of the sociocultural landscape, which seems to be the view adopted by the Appalachian Trail's founding father, Benton MacKaye. MacKaye proposed an initial project in regional planning that he hoped would bridge the gap between two spheres that traditionally had remained separate—wilderness preservation and community life (Minteer 2001). MacKaye did not offer a utopia of escape found in the wilderness but rather a "complex examination of the values of the American social and political community and its relationship with the natural environment" (Minteer 2001, 192).

MacKaye's project in regional planning contained four components, all of which were volunteer based, not for profit, and constructed and maintained in the spirit of cooperation (MacKaye 1921):

> the Appalachian Trail—a service trail or path between shelter camps, divided into sections and maintained by a local group, and dotted with lookout stations for forest fires;
> shelter camps—accommodations for sleeping (sometimes eating), spaced apart for a comfortable day's trek and regulated so as not to be abused;
> community groups—small communities on or near the trail used for nonindustrial activities; and
> food and farm camps—supplements to community camps and offering possible sources for new and healthy employment in the outdoors (e.g., farming, forestry).

Rather than serving strictly as a resource to critique industrialism, MacKaye's vision was to serve as more of a practical solution for the "encroachment of socially and environmentally destructive metropolitan forces into authentic rural communities" (Minteer 2001, 193). MacKaye's new domain was neither urban nor rural but incorporated dimensions of both spheres. This new socioeconomic realm would be restructured in such a way that need, not profit, would drive economic activity, and communitarian ideologies would influence and shape social relationships (Foresta 1987). The object of the Appalachian Trail project was to develop indigenous America so that both the countryside and community could thrive.

Most of the areas designated national parks during the early twentieth century, such as Yellowstone and Yosemite, were located in the western states, but MacKaye (1921) proposed that camping grounds were of particular use to people living in dense population centers, most of which happened to be in the east. The Appalachian Mountains, for most of the eastern population, were no more than a day's drive away and thus a perfect base for both work and play. MacKaye expected that families and individuals would come to the Appalachians for short vacations in the outdoors (Foresta 1987). These minivacations would allow visitors to gain perspective on the social context in which they lived and worked in metropolitan areas. MacKaye thought these vacation communities would develop around shelter areas on the trail and eventually become permanent exchange-based socioeconomic communities (Foresta 1987). The economy of these communities would be based on farming, forestry, and local manufacturing and become an alternative to urban industrialized society. MacKaye was not anti-urban or against industry but believed the urban could be incorporated into a balanced regional landscape (Foresta 1987).

MacKaye's devotion to the Appalachian Trail project was guided by a humanitarian motive: he hoped to help individuals achieve better living conditions. In the language of social constructionism, Benton MacKaye was a moral entrepreneur (Becker 1973), a crusading reformer dissatisfied with life as it currently existed. As he saw it, a recreational camp and community life, compared to a growing capitalist industrial society, would eventually replace the dull, standardized existence of the urban working class and become a sanctuary and refuge from the commercialism of everyday life (MacKaye 1921; Minteer 2001).

MacKaye also believed that the transformative value of experiences in the natural world would lead people to question and reject consumption and materialism. As we know, however, the Appalachian Trail did not become the instrument of social reform he envisioned. While industrialism was in the process of contributing to the urban growth and rural decay that bothered social reformers like MacKaye, a more secure, privileged group of modern professionals was emerging who were catered to by both industry and government and did not directly experience the negatives of industrialization. Due to the nature of their work, these professionals— who included public land managers, foresters, lawyers, professors, physicians, editors, scientists—often experienced upward mobility and a level of individuality made possible by comfortable incomes (Foresta 1987). Professionals benefitted from the rise of industrial capitalism because this new world was becoming increasingly technology-based, educated, and dependent on professional services. With such upwardly mobile professionals at the helm of the Appalachian Trail project, it was used for their interests, as those in positions of power often have the ability and influence to do. This group viewed the Appalachian Trail as a recreational site that provided the middle class a temporary escape from the pressures of society rather than as a permanent alternative to life for the urban working class. From what I observed when hiking the Appalachian Trail, such remains the case today. As may be recalled from chapter 2, many hike the trail as a way of escape, and the majority of those who do hike have the economic means necessary to remove themselves from daily responsibilities and the working world, at least for a short time.

Perhaps MacKaye was one of the first to illustrate the extent to which a recreational trail is a symbolic environment, a socially constructed natural (and in this case, national) landscape. According to Ronald Foresta, "The aura of success about the Trail is a reminder of this potential and of the degree to which a sensibly arranged landscape is a social artifact" (1987, 85). In contrast, or rather in addition to essentialist and constructionist views regarding wilderness, Brian Fay (2003) suggests that meanings comprising landscapes, given a variety of possibilities, are created through social interaction and negotiation. This makes sense. As we cope with a new environment, we change it and in the process are changed by it because nature and society are interrelated (Nordquist 2006). As a result of hikers' experiences and interactions in this new environment over an extended period of time, the Appalachian Trail becomes an expression of hikers' personalities, a significant part of who they are. Simply stated, place matters. Becoming aware of relationships between humans and natural environments in this manner, and focusing specifically on the significance of place, allows us to gain a better understanding regarding cultural expressions that long-distance hikers use to define who they were, are, and hope to become.

Leisure subcultures and subcultural identities maintain a delicate balance between difference and sameness with respect to larger society. Whereas countercultures are characterized as rejecting or distancing themselves from mainstream culture, subcultures selectively borrow from mainstream culture, often twisting certain aspects to suit their own purposes. The same is true of hikers on the Appalachian Trail: as members of this leisure subculture, they negotiate mainstream cultural values, and articulate their views and define their distinctive identities using key aspects of American culture. For example, although long-distance hikers reject material consumption and consumerism, viewing both as societal negatives, they actively embrace the consumption of nature and leisure. Of course, there are many reasons offered for these new forms of consumption, from being tired of a current job to wanting a break before starting a career or family, from searching for answers or for God to dealing with a loss or personal issue that needs to be resolved. For numerous reasons, people remove themselves from society to seek refuge in the wilderness. The uncivilizing process that begins when hikers leave home for the healing properties of the Appalachian Trail seems to provide hikers with an escape that they otherwise would not find at home or through work. There is something telling or romantic about leaving life and family behind to retreat into the wilderness to find oneself. With the multiple identities and roles we take on in society, people may feel as if their identities are becoming more and more fragmented. So they head to the Appalachian Trail, back to nature, removing themselves from society in hope of finding a more authentic self.

The hiking mantra "Hike your own hike" suggests that hikers embrace the core American value of individualism. And they do. Since there are many ways to hike the trail, this phrase also implies that individuals should hike and are free to hike the Appalachian Trail in any way they choose. After all, only you can hike your hike, right? No one else can do this, be it mentally or physically. By our nature, however, we are social beings, and despite needing to get away from the rat race or distractions at home and work, hikers get lonely and at times need encouragement from others, both on and off the trail, to continue on their way. In fact, that social aspect—the hiking community—is what many remember most about their hike on the Appalachian Trail. Even though long-distance hiking is a solo activity, there is something very communal about the trail experience, especially when the experiences and memories can be shared with others who understand.

Perhaps this is one reason why, in spite of the differences that emerge among hikers, a place referent mediates, and members of the hiking community view one another as equals. We would do well to learn from hikers that difference does not always lead to inequality or the unequal treatment of others. The uncivilizing process that occurs as people hike the Appalachian Trail seems to break down many societal barriers, making us more sociable, and more trusting of and accountable to others, despite real or perceived differences among us.

For MacKaye, the transformation of the Appalachian Trail from an instrument of social reform to a recreational facility illustrated what is sometimes a fortunate, and sometimes an unfortunate, vision—that of rearranging landscapes to address the shortcomings of modern life (Foresta 1987). I am not so sure MacKaye would be disappointed in what the AT has come to mean and symbolize for long-distance hikers and outdoor enthusiasts today. His original vision for the Appalachian Trail was one that combined opportunities for recreation, recuperation, and employment. Something certainly happens as hikers remove themselves from society, stripping down to the bare minimum to search for a simpler life, if only temporarily. Maybe it is the opportunity to engage in a recreational activity, or to recuperate as MacKaye wanted, with or without work involved. All I can say is this: for those willing to join the hiking community and take a walk on the wild side, the Appalachian Trail is a pretty special place in which to do it. But don't take my word for it. As North Florida Swamp Donkey explained, "The pain in the ass the trail is makes it to where there are only so many people that will do it. If it was real easy, then everybody would do it and there'd be nothing special about it." Many long-distance hikers will find that their experiences mirror those found within these pages and some won't. In the end, I have attempted to highlight the contours of this leisure subculture and describe life on the Appalachian Trail as it is for long-distance hikers.

APPENDIX
RESEARCH METHODOLOGY

In this study, I have used two different data sources—ethnographic field-notes and qualitative interviews. The methods used to collect and analyze these data are described briefly below.

OBSERVATIONAL FIELDWORK AND IN-DEPTH INTERVIEWS

An Ethnographic Perspective

Data collection activities for this project—fieldwork, participant observation, and semistructured qualitative interviews—took place in two waves on various sections of the Appalachian Trail. During the summer of 2005, I spent 32 days on the Appalachian Trail hiking 330 miles between North Carolina and Virginia. I spent 22 days on the trail during the summer of 2007 and hiked approximately 250 miles between Virginia and Pennsylvania. In mid-May of both 2005 and 2007, I attended the annual Trail Days Festival in Damascus, Virginia, along with approximately 10,000 people (locals, hiking enthusiasts, current and former AT hikers, gear representatives, and the like).

To examine more fully how the long-distance hiking subculture on the Appalachian Trail is constructed and negotiated among long-distance hikers, I conducted extensive ethnographic fieldwork to observe and record interactions among long-distance hikers and between hikers and nonhikers (such as trail angels, local community members, and members of religious congregations), while observing and recording my own experiences and interactions with others along the trail. Such fieldwork is designed to explore the "accomplishments" and constructed character of ongoing social interaction. As I immersed myself in the ongoing social activities of the long-distance hiking subculture, I was mindful to look for recurring themes or patterns in behavior or action that were, and perhaps were not, happening in this environment. I was also conscious of the ways long-distance hikers drew symbolic boundaries between themselves and relevant reference groups. My observations of the long-distance hiking community on the Appalachian Trail have been recorded in approximately two hundred pages of fieldnotes.

During this process, in-depth interviews were also conducted with 46 men and women on the Appalachian Trail who identified themselves as long-distance hikers (that is, section hikers or thru-hikers). It is important to note that 9 of the interviews were conducted by a second researcher during the summer of 2005. The first few interviews conducted by the second researcher occurred in my presence to ensure that the process would be uniform and the data would be collected as indicated in my original research proposal. In the selection of interviewees, a purposive sampling technique was employed. Because previously reviewed literature (Kyle et al. 2003) indicated that thru-hikers and section hikers on the Appalachian Trail interact with the trail in more meaningful ways than do other types of hikers, I did not approach day hikers and weekend/overnight hikers. More specifically, hikers were selected based on the amount of time they had been hiking on the Appalachian Trail (at least four weeks of continuous hiking), as well as on their availability and willingness to participate. No one I approached declined to be interviewed. The interviews were conducted in a semistructured fashion, meaning each respondent had the opportunity to answer every question. Unanticipated topics that surfaced during the interview were pursued further through follow-up questions not originally included in the interview questionnaire.

Interview sites included, but were not limited to, shelters (three-wall lean-tos), restaurants or libraries in local communities, and hiker hostels, all of which are found along or near the trail. Most interviews, however, were conducted in the evenings at trail shelters or during Trail Days in Damascus. I often talked and interacted with these same people in other contexts as a participant observer, namely, when we ate in the evenings at the shelters or throughout the day along the trail. Each interview was recorded on audiotape and lasted anywhere from forty-five to ninety minutes, yielding 357 pages of interview transcripts. Additional notes were taken after the interview to enhance the analysis of recorded accounts. Trail names, rather than pseudonyms, are used when presenting the results of this study because they are a key element of the long-distance hiking sub-culture. Trail names provide anonymity in this context and are used and published with permission by the participants.

It is important to recognize that the hikers interviewed are in no way representative of all types of hikers along the Appalachian Trail, given that nearly four million people will set foot on the trail each year, nor are long-distance hikers a homogenous group. In other words, the perspectives that emerged from these interviews are not expected or intended to be exhaustive of all possible viewpoints of those who make up the long-distance hiking community. My goal was to recount the various standpoints (e.g., perceptions), strategies (e.g., motivations, goals, behaviors), and stories (e.g., narratives) used by long-distance hikers to reflect upon and understand their experiences on the Appalachian Trail, and to situate such standpoints in their proper social context rather than generalizing from their accounts. This coding scheme was communicated through personal contact in a seminar course, Qualitative Analysis, taken during the summer of 2004. I am indebted to Dr. John P. Bartkowski for sharing this approach.

Once recorded and transcribed, interview transcripts and fieldnotes were analyzed with a range of topics in mind, including the following: day-to-day life on the Appalachian Trail; similarities between religious pilgrimage and long-distance hiking or backpacking; the giving, receiving, and meaning of trail names; experiences with trail magic; encounters with trail angels; general hiking experiences; expectations prior to hiking; visits to local communities; relationships and interactions with fellow hikers, as well as locals when in town; highest and lowest points while hiking the trail; and the effect of "reentry" or transitioning back home for hikers after trail life is over, among other topics explored. Topics chosen for my interview questionnaire were informed by my personal hiking experiences on the Appalachian Trail. Beginning May 1, 1999, I spent 40 days hiking 350 miles of the Appalachian Trail from the Delaware Water Gap Recreation Area on the Pennsylvania–New Jersey border to Manchester Center, Vermont. I have section-hiked approximately two-thirds of the Appalachian Trail to date. (These and other topics investigated are presented in the interview questionnaire reprinted at the end of this appendix.)

When analyzing fieldnotes and interview transcripts, I also paid attention to emergent themes to capture other issues that surfaced apart from those mentioned above. Additionally, I identified narratives, including storylines, images, and metaphors, used by long-distance hikers to engage members and distinguish themselves from relevant reference groups. And, of course, the data were analyzed with the theoretical concepts from chapter 1 in mind (namely, social identity theory, subcultural theory, and boundary work). I intentionally did not analyze interview responses on a question-by-question basis. To do so would be a disservice to the participants in this study.

Consistent with ethnographic convention, my goal was "to place specific encounters, events, and understandings into a fuller, more meaningful context" (Denzin and Lincoln 2000, 455). I engaged in this level of fieldwork, rather than resting on assumptions, because this intimate, interpersonal approach allowed me to recount the everyday lived experiences of long-distance hikers. Furthermore, folding interview accounts together with those emerging from observational research allowed me to render a rich, complex portrait of the hiking community on the Appalachian Trail. For example, in-depth interviews allowed hikers to share their experiences on the Appalachian Trail with me. At the same time, ethnographic fieldwork allowed me to further examine and understand these experiences firsthand. Had I not spent weeks in the field hiking with them, I would not have been able to fully understand or experience what sociologist Emile Durkheim meant by "collective effervescence" or the intense emotional feeling that is generated when members of the hiking community come together, particularly at events like Trail Days. Collective effervescence allows hikers to recharge their batteries and reaffirm their social bonds, when the community comes together, even if for a short time. When the festival is over, hikers resume their individual journeys on the Appalachian Trail until the next communal gathering that will allow them to move as a group beyond themselves. By integrating interview data with that gained from participant observation, I was better able to understand how a long-distance hiking subculture was constructed and negotiated among long-distance hikers, both on and off the trail. Use of only a single method of inquiry or of a qualitative software program would not have allowed me to gain such an in-depth understanding of the situated behaviors and everyday practices of long-distance hikers.

Interview Sample Characteristics

Of the 46 long-distance hikers interviewed, 9 were thru-hiking the Appalachian Trail for the second time, and in at least four cases, the third time. In fact, the overwhelming majority of long-distance hikers interviewed identified themselves as thru-hikers, even if this was their first attempt at a thru-hike. Most had begun hiking the Appalachian Trail in mid- to late March or early April. While April Fool's Day is the traditional day for starting a northbound thru-hike, a few of the long-distance hikers interviewed had started as early as February. All participants, with the exception of three, had been hiking the trail for four or more weeks when interviewed. One had only been on the trail for two weeks at the time of the interview but planned on hiking five hundred miles. A young couple whose car broke down on the way to Jazz Fest in New Orleans decided to hike back to Connecticut and had been on the trail almost three weeks when interviewed. Forty-one of the interviews were conducted individually, while two married couples were interviewed together.

All participants were high school graduates, and nearly two-thirds indicated they had received a college degree, including two-year, four-year, and graduate degrees. One-third indicated they had attended some college. The most common occupations held by long-distance hikers were professional or career jobs (for example, nurse, teacher, police officer, ordained minister, graphic designer, deputy auditor general for Navajo Nation, music and film production) or service/retail jobs (for example, restaurant server, bartender, retail employee, group home assistant, photographer's assistant). The Appalachian Trail runs along the eastern portion of the United States, so it was not surprising that most of the hikers interviewed were from this area, representing nine of the fourteen states that make up the trail corridor. Other hikers were from the midwestern, southwestern, or western regions of the country; two were from outside of the United States (Canada, Israel).

Slightly more than half of the long-distance hikers interviewed were male. The majority of long-distance hikers interviewed were between the ages of twenty-two and thirty-five. Other age concentrations included individuals fifty-one or older or those younger than twenty-two years of age. Unfortunately, there is a lack of racial diversity on the trail. All participants' observed race was recorded as white.

TABLE 1.   In-Depth Interview Questionnaire

Demographic Information and Previous Hiking Experience

1. Hometown
2. Age
3. Race
4. Gender
5. Highest degree received and college major (if applicable)
6. Current or most recent occupation
7. Parent or primary care giver's total years of education
8. Parents' current or most recent occupation
9. Previous long-distance hiking experience elsewhere. Where? When? For how long? How old were you at the time?

General Questions about AT Experience

1. Previous hiking experience on the AT
2. When did you begin your hike on the AT?
3. Why did you decide to hike the AT?
   a. What have other hikers told you about their decisions to begin hiking the AT? Were they similar to or different from yours? In what way(s)?
   b. What do you like most about the trail? What do you like least about the trail?
   c. Is there anything in general you would change about the trail? Tell me about this. PROBE (if needed): regarding shelters, local communities, safety, fellow hikers, trail names, trail magic, physical or emotional challenges
4. Tell me about your trail name.
   a. How did it come about? Who gave it to you? Why? What does this name say about you?
   b. In your opinion, what is the significance of trail names? What does it add or take away from the overall hiking experience on the AT?

Daily Life on the AT

5. Describe your average day to me.
   a. What did you expect or imagine this experience would be like? Were these expectations met? If not, why? PROBE (if needed): regarding shelters, local communities, safety, fellow hikers, trail names, trail magic, physical or emotional challenges
   b. Are there certain characteristics shared by long-distance hikers? If so, please tell me about this. PROBE (if needed): physically, mentally, emotionally, career-wise, financially

TABLE 1. *(continued)*

Daily Life on the AT

6. Sometimes the AT may take you nearby or through a local community. Describe your experiences in local communities.
   a. How did this experience make you feel? What have other hikers told you about this? PROBE (if needed) in comparison to trail life, similarities and differences in environment, interactions with locals versus interactions with fellow hikers
7. Sometimes hikers speak of something called "trail magic." Have you heard of this? If so, please describe what this is exactly.
   a. Have you personally been the recipient of or been responsible for bringing trail magic to another? Please describe.
   b. Do you know of any other hikers who have experienced trail magic? What have others told you about this? Please describe.
   c. What is the interaction like with other hikers? What role do other hikers play in terms of your own experience?

Memorable Experiences

8. Thinking back over the time you have spent hiking the AT, what would you say has been your most memorable experience involving your surroundings or the natural environment? Why this experience?
9. Thinking back over the time you have spent hiking the AT, what would you say has been the highest point for you? What did you learn from this experience?
   a. What has been your most challenging experience? What did you take away from this experience?
   b. What have you learned about yourself since you began your hike?
10. Is there anything I did not ask that you feel is important in terms of understanding the AT experience or your personal experience on the AT?

REFERENCES

Appalachian Trail Conservancy. 2008. "2,000-Milers: Facts and Statistics." Accessed
March 28. http://www.appalachiantrail.org/site/c.jkLXJ8MQKtH/b.851143/.

Becker, Howard S. 1973. *Outsiders: Studies in the Sociology of Deviance.* New York: Free
Press.

Bradley, Graham L. 2010. "Skate Parks as a Context for Adolescent Development."
Journal of Adolescent Research 25: 288–323.

Bright-Fey, John. 2004. *Tao Te Ching: An Authentic Taoist Translation.* Raleigh, NC:
Sweetwater Press.

Bruce, Dan "Wingfoot." 2006. *The Thru-hiker's Handbook.* 16th ed. Hot Springs, NC:
Center for Appalachian Trail Studies.

Bryson, Bill. 1998. *A Walk in the Woods: Rediscovering America on the Appalachian Trail.*
New York: Crown Publishing Group.

Chazin, Daniel D. 2013. *Appalachian Trail Data Book.* 35th ed. Harper's Ferry, WV:
Appalachian Trail Conservancy.

Cohen, Erik. 2003. "Backpacking: Diversity and Change." *Journal of Tourism and Cultural Change* 1(2): 95–110.

Cohen, Scott A. 2011. "Lifestyle Travellers: Backpacking as a Way of Life." *Annals of
Tourism Research* 38(4): 1535–1555.

Dant, Tim, and Belinda Wheaton. 2007. "Windsurfing: An Extreme Form of Material
and Embodied Interaction?" *Anthropology Today* 23(6): 8–12.

Denzin, Norman K., and Yvonna S. Lincoln. 2000. *Handbook of Qualitative Research.*
2nd ed. Thousand Oaks, CA: Sage Publications.

Eberhart, M. J. 2007. *Ten Million Steps: Nimblewill Nomad's Epic 10-Month Trek from
the Florida Keys to Quebec.* Birmingham, AL: Menasha Ridge Press.

Elias, Norbert. 2000. *The Civilizing Process.* Rev. ed. Oxford: Blackwell Publishing.

Erikson, Kai. 1994. *A New Species of Trouble: The Human Experience of Modern Disasters.* New York: W. W. Norton.

Fay, Brian. 2003. "Introduction: Environmental History: Nature at Work." *History and
Theory* 42(4): 1–4.

Foresta, Ronald. 1987. "Transformation of the Appalachian Trail." *Geographical Review*
77(1): 76–85.

Garvey, Edward B. 1971. *Appalachian Hiker: Adventure of a Lifetime.* 3rd ed. Oakton,
VA: Appalachian Books.

Gelder, Ken. 2007. *Subcultures: Cultural Histories and Social Practice.* New York:
Routledge.

Greider, Thomas, and Lorraine Garkovich. 1994. "Landscapes: The Social Construction of Nature and the Environment." *Rural Sociology* 59(1): 1–24.

Griswold, Wendy. 2008. *Cultures and Societies in a Changing World.* 3rd ed. Thousand Oaks, CA: Pine Forge Press.

Holyfield, Lori, and Lilian Jonas. 2003. "From River God to Research Grunt: Identity, Emotions, and the River Guide." *Symbolic Interaction* 26(2): 285–306.

Hunt, Jennifer C. 1995. "Divers' Accounts of Normal Risk." *Symbolic Interaction* 18(4): 439–462.

Irving, Washington. 2008. *The Legend of Sleepy Hollow and Other Stories.* Mineola, NY: Dover Publications.

Jenkins, Peter. 2001. *A Walk across America.* New York: William Morrow Paperbacks.

Jusdanis, Gregory. 1987. *The Poetics of Cavafy: Textuality, Eroticism, History.* Princeton: Princeton University Press.

Kerouac, Jack. 1958. *The Dharma Bums.* New York: Penguin Books.

Kyle, Gerard, Kelly Bricker, Alan Graefe, and Thomas Wickham. 2004. "An Examination of Recreationists' Relationships with Activities and Settings." *Leisure Sciences* 26: 123–142.

Kyle, Gerard, Alan Graefe, Robert Manning, and James Bacon. 2003. "An Examination of the Relationship between Leisure Activity Involvement and Place Attachment among Hikers along the Appalachian Trail." *Journal of Leisure Research* 35(3): 249–273.

———. 2004. "Predictors of Behavioral Loyalty among Hikers along the Appalachian Trail." *Leisure Sciences* 26: 99–118.

Lamont, Michele. 1992. *Money, Morals, and Manners: The Culture of the French and American Upper-Middle Class.* Chicago: University of Chicago Press.

———. 2000. *The Dignity of Working Men: Morality and the Boundaries of Race, Class, and Immigration.* New York: Russell Sage Foundation.

Luxenberg, Larry. 1994. *Walking the Appalachian Trail.* Mechanicsburg, PA: Stackpole Books.

MacKaye, Benton. 1921. "An Appalachian Trail: A Project in Regional Planning." *Journal of the American Institute of Architects* 9: 325–330.

Manning, Robert, William Valliere, James Bacon, Alan Graefe, Gerard Kyle, and Rita Hennessey. 2000. "Use and Users of the Appalachian Trail: A Source Book." Accessed April 3, 2006. http://www.nps.gov/applications/parks/appa/ppdocuments/Main_Report.pdf.

Miller, David "Awol." 2013. *The A.T. Guide Northbound 2013.* Titusville, FL: Jerelyn Press.

Minteer, Ben A. 2001. "Wilderness and the Wise Province: Benton MacKaye's Pragmatic Vision." *Philosophy and Geography* 4(2): 185–202.

Mueser, Roland. 1998. *Long-Distance Hiking: Lessons from the Appalachian Trail.* Camden, ME: International Marine/Ragged Mountain Press.

Nordquist, Michael. 2006. "The End of Nature and Society: Bruno Latour and the Nonhuman in Politics." Accessed March 28, 2008. http://www.allacademic.com/meta/p_mla_apa_research_citation/0/9/7/2/5/p97253_index.html.

Proshansky, Harold M. 1978. "The City and Self-Identity." *Environment and Behavior* 10: 147–169.

Shaffer, Tracy Stephenson. 2004. "Performing Backpacking: Constructing 'Authenticity' Every Step of the Way." *Text and Performance Quarterly* 24(2): 139–160.

Stets, Jan E., and Peter J. Burke. 2000. "Identity Theory and Social Identity Theory." *Social Psychology Quarterly* 63: 224–237.

Strayed, Cheryl. 2012. *Wild: From Lost to Found on the Pacific Crest Trail*. New York: Knopf.

Stryker, Sheldon. 1991. "Exploring the Relevance of Social Cognition for the Relationship of Self and Society: Linking the Cognitive Perspective and Identity Theory." In *The Self-Society Dynamic: Cognition, Emotion, and Action*, edited by Judith A. Howard and Peter L. Callero, 19–41. Cambridge: Cambridge University Press.

Stryker, Sheldon, and Richard T. Serpe. 1982. "Commitment, Identity Salience, and Role Behavior: A Theory and Research Example." In *Personality, Roles, and Social Behavior*, edited by William Ickes and Eric S. Knowles, 199–218. New York: Springer-Verlag.

Tajfel, Henri. 1970. "Experiments in Intergroup Discrimination." *Scientific American* 223: 96–102.

Tajfel, Henri, and John C. Turner. 1986. "The Social Identity Theory of Intergroup Behavior." In *Psychology of Intergroup Relations*, 2nd ed., edited by S. Worchel and W. G. Austin, 7–24. Chicago: Nelson-Hall.

Turner, John C., Penelope J. Oakes, S. Alexander Haslam, and Craig McGarty. 1994. "Self and Collective: Cognition and Social Context." *Personality and Social Psychology Bulletin* 20(5): 454–463.

Turner, Victor. 1974. *Dramas, Fields, and Metaphors: Symbolic Action in Human Society*. Ithaca, NY: Cornell University Press.

United States Forest Service, Department of Agriculture. 1982. "ROS Users Guide." Accessed December 1, 2014. http://www.fs.fed.us/cdt/carrying_capacity/rosguide_1982.pdf.

Wheaton, Belinda. 2000. "'Just Do It': Consumption, Commitment, and Identity in the Windsurfing Subculture." *Sociology of Sport Journal* 17: 254–274.

Wheaton, Belinda, and Becky Beal. 2003. "'Keeping It Real.'" *International Review for the Sociology of Sport* 38(2): 155–176.

Wheaton, Belinda, and Alan Tomlinson. 1998. "The Changing Gender Order in Sport? The Case of Windsurfing Subcultures." *Journal of Sport and Social Issues* 22(3): 252–274.

Williams, Trevor, and Peter Donnelly. 1985. "Subcultural Production, Reproduction, and Transformation in Climbing." *International Review for the Sociology of Sport* 20(1–2): 3–17.

INDEX

*Indicates trail names

ABOUT THE AUTHOR

KRISTI M. FONDREN is an associate professor of sociology at Marshall University in Huntington, West Virginia. She has spent many years researching topics in the areas of sports, recreation, and leisure. Her work has been published in a variety of journals, including *Gender Issues, Journal of Issues in Intercollegiate Athletics*, and *Review of Religious Research*. Since 1999 she has hiked more than 1,700 miles of the Appalachian Trail and has presented widely at professional meetings, both national and regional, on the subject of long-distance hiking.

CPSIA information can be obtained at www.ICGtesting.com
Printed in the USA
BVOW08s0208071215

429527BV00002B/6/P

9 780813 571881